COMMON SENSE

ASSESSMENT

in the

CLASSROOM

Author
Lynda Rice, M.Ed.

SHELL EDUCATION

Publishing Credits

Dona Herweck Rice, *Editor-in-Chief*; Robin Erickson, *Production Director*;
Lee Aucoin, *Creative Director*; Sara Johnson, M.S.Ed., *Senior Editor*;
Leah Quillian, *Assistant Editor*; Emily Engle, *Editor*; Grace Alba, *Designer*;
Corinne Burton, M.A.Ed., *Publisher*

Shell Education

5301 Oceanus Drive
Huntington Beach, CA 92649-1030
http://www.shelleducation.com

ISBN 978-1-4258-0690-3

© 2013 Shell Educational Publishing, Inc.

COMMON SENSE ASSESSMENT *in the* CLASSROOM

Table of Contents

Foreword

All educators need to be thoroughly familiar with the concepts and the strategies involved in assessing student content knowledge. Assessment informs current and future teaching and learning, serving as the basis on which many educational decisions are made. And educators are well aware of this; the vast majority agree that assessing their own teaching and their students' learning are vital parts of what they do. Yet despite this, many educators find it difficult to implement effective assessment in the classroom. For many teachers, there is a gap between what they believe assessment should be like and how it actually happens in the classroom. Lynda Rice's *Common Sense Assessment in the Classroom* offers educators a very practical, or "common sense," approach to bridging that gap and applying the assessment strategies in their classrooms. This is shown throughout the book in several ways. Rice's conversational tone, for example, engages readers, inviting them to adopt the common sense approach as they read both the research and personal anecdotes that support the assessment strategies presented.

Common Sense Assessment in the Classroom is based on the premise that each student learns differently. The research-based argument is that since we think and express knowledge differently, assessment should reflect those differences. Throughout the book, Rice demonstrates that assessment should take many forms and that both educators and their students benefit when they broaden their perspective about how assessment should work.

Each of the six chapters focuses on one aspect of assessment. For instance, one is dedicated to pre-assessment, another to formative assessment, and another to summative assessment. In each chapter, Rice offers readers informative definitions and descriptions to provide background. She also suggests ways that teachers can implement a wide variety of pre-assessments, formative assessments, and summative assessments in their classrooms. Those assessments are discussed in more detail in later chapters as Rice describes more formal evaluation procedures, including final grading and reporting. Each chapter contains examples and templates that teachers can adapt to fit the needs of their students. Teachers who have wondered how to put together and use meaningful assessments will be glad to see the examples Rice offers.

"Review and Reflect Questions" appear at the end of each chapter, allowing readers to apply the concepts discussed to their own teaching contexts.

Common Sense Assessment in the Classroom is a useful guide and resource for the busy teacher who is looking for ways to more effectively assess students. The templates, examples, and practical advice Rice offers for implementing assessment in day-to-day classroom activities are second to none, providing teachers with the resources they need to purposefully modify their instruction. Readers who expect the discussion of classroom assessment to be dry and removed from the reality of classroom life can think again—*Common Sense Assessment in the Classroom* makes assessing students meaningful again, engaging the reader with upbeat language and most importantly with strategies that work!

—Margot Kinberg, Ph.D.
Associate Professor and author

Acknowledgments

The success of any project depends largely on the encouragement of the people around you. So I want to take this opportunity to express my gratitude to the people who inspired me to create and complete this book.

My greatest appreciation goes to Dr. Paul Shepherd, a dear friend, colleague, former principal, and educational consultant. As I worked to put my feelings and thoughts into words and eventually onto these pages, my conversations with Dr. Shepherd helped me to hone those words into the common-sense voice that defines this book. Thank you, Paul, for your tremendous support and inspiration.

I also want to thank the teachers who have attended my workshops and seminars over the years. I am grateful to them for sharing their successes and struggles with assessment and grading in their own classrooms. The professional collaboration with those passionate teachers who are always looking for a better way has given me the "meat" I needed to make this book a practical how-to manual for today's classrooms.

I also want to thank Keslie and Tim Lyons for keeping their coffee shop open for me when I needed to escape my office for a new environment, which, in turn, brought forth new perspectives on my ideas and my writing.

The guidance and support received from all of these people was vital for the success of this book. I am grateful for their unwavering assistance and support.

Preface

As a child, after being reprimanded by my mother, I remember saying, "I will never say that to my child when I grow up!" Lo and behold, I grew up and I did say those things to my children, word for word. I'd slap my hand over my mouth and realize I had become my mother. In defense of my mother, as a parent myself, I now see why she said those things. I felt justified!

The same went for me when I was in school. When I received a grade that I thought was not fair or when the teacher would hold a test score over my head as leverage to make me do better, I remember saying, "If I were a teacher, I would never do that!" Lo and behold, I did become a teacher. And I did do those things. I'd slap my hand over my mouth and realize I had become my teachers. In defense of my teachers, as a teacher myself, I saw why they said and did those things. But I did not feel justified this time. Each time that I panicked and fell back on those tactics that I despised as a student, I couldn't help but think that there must be a better way.

My own children would come home from school, distraught about a grade they had received on an assignment or a test. Some of their comments were, "I got a C because I didn't finish," or, "I didn't put my name on my paper, so I lost 10 points," or, "Jamie didn't do his part on our project, so I had to do the whole thing," or, "I knew the stuff, but I hate tests, so I got a D." Etc., etc., etc. These comments stuck with me because I had uttered them as a student, and now my children were uttering them. Now I am a teacher, and I hear my students uttering them.

Unwittingly, I perpetuated the *Whadja Get? Syndrome.* Unwittingly, I used grades as punishment by saying, "You didn't turn in your homework, so you get a zero." Unwittingly, I struck fear into the hearts of my students with the warning, "If you get a low score on one assignment, it will drag the average down a whole grade on your report card." I meant no harm, but with these comments, I put the focus on the grade, not the work or the process of improvement. As a result, to my horror, when I returned graded assignments back to the students, they would turn to each other immediately and say, "Whadja get?" Not, as I would hope, "Which ones did you miss? How did this happen? What do I need to do to fix this?" Rather, "Whadja get?"

Do you ever have an uncomfortable feeling in the pit of your stomach when you are grading papers, assigning grades, or administering tests? A feeling that is telling you that what you are doing just isn't right? Pay attention to that feeling. That is your common sense crying out *Wait a minute! This doesn't make sense! This isn't fair! This doesn't work to help this student be successful! This doesn't help me to be a better teacher!* When your common sense tells you to do something differently, listen to it.

I do believe that we as educators are all doing the best we can by our students with the information we have at that time. I have no doubt that all of my teachers did and said everything with the very best of intentions. In my case, when it came to assessing and grading fairly, I did not know what else to do, as my role models were the teachers I'd had in years gone by. And their role models were their teachers. And on and on. So each time I engaged in a practice that reminded me of what was not fair or did not make sense, I knew it was time to replace the old information with a new and improved version. In this case, I needed a new way to look at assessment and grading in my classroom.

As educators, we all have the same goal: to help our students make the maximum possible academic gains in a positive, respectful environment that promotes their success and nurtures their desire to learn. One of the greatest tools available to us in this pursuit is using common sense when applying new research to our classroom practices. It's important to continue to learn, attend workshops, read the research, and then sift through this new information with your common sense filter as you apply these ideas in your practice.

Navigating the Text

The chapters in this book are organized so as to mirror the path of assessment that you take with your students. **Chapter 1** focuses on what common sense assessment means and the essential qualities of common sense assessment practices. **Chapter 2** begins the journey of assessment in your classroom by highlighting the importance of pre-assessment and how to pre-assess students for their learning modalities and readiness for academic content. **Chapter 3** continues on the path of instruction by discussing common sense practices for formative assessment and how to gather useful information as your students practice with and move toward mastery of the standards. **Chapter 4** makes the leap from formative assessment (practice) to summative assessment (final shows of mastery). The chapter discusses a variety of methods for administering summative assessments. **Chapter 5** introduces ideas on how to evaluate, grade, and keep track of summative assessment scores in a standards-based system, including final grades and progress reports. And finally, **Chapter 6** helps you take the first steps to applying the strategies discussed throughout the book by helping you evaluate your own assessment practices and empowering you to make positive changes.

Conclusion

This book was born out of my passion for teaching and doing right by my students and fellow teachers. I am excited to share my understanding of authentic assessment and how it can be used, not for leverage to frighten students into doing better, but for diagnosing problem areas, prescribing learning pathways, and driving future instruction. (I am excited to share productive ways to grade and report that are fair and will help track student progress over time.) By applying the common sense strategies in this book, we can replace the *Whadja Get? Syndrome* with the *Whadja Learn? Legacy*.

As you read these chapters and review the samples and suggested strategies, you will find that they may reinforce much of what you already know and do. Or you may be introduced to a practice that you are not using but could integrate into your current routine. In either case, I hope this book will help expand your knowledge of effective assessment and grading practices. With deep respect, I thank you for your dedication to children and our shared profession.

—Lynda

Barnes & Noble Booksellers #2138
150 Silhavy Road Suite 120
Valparaiso, IN 46383
219-531-6551

STR:2138 REG:003 TRN:4182 CSHR:Stephanie B

EDUCATOR   EXP: 09/24/2017

Common Sense Assessment in the Classroom
   9781425806903   T1
   (1 @ 21.99) Educator 20% (4.40)
   (1 @ 17.59)   17.59

Subtotal   17.59
Sales Tax T1 (7.000%)   1.23
TOTAL   18.82
MASTERCARD DEBIT   18.82
   Card#: XXXXXXXXXXXXX0103

Thanks for shopping at
Barnes & Noble

101.39A   05/15/2016 01:20PM

CUSTOMER COPY

With a sales receipt or Barnes & Noble.com packing slip, a full refund in the original form of payment will be issued from any Barnes & Noble Booksellers store for returns of undamaged NOOKs, new and unread books, and unopened and undamaged music CDs, DVDs, vinyl records, toys/games and audio books made within 14 days of purchase from a Barnes & Noble Booksellers store or Barnes & Noble.com with the below exceptions:

A store credit for the purchase price will be issued (i) for purchases made by check less than 7 days prior to the date of return, (ii) when a gift receipt is presented within 60 days of purchase, (iii) for textbooks, (iv) when the original tender is PayPal, or (v) for products purchased at Barnes & Noble College bookstores that are listed for sale in the Barnes & Noble Booksellers inventory management system.

Opened music CDs, DVDs, vinyl records, audio books may not be returned, and can be exchanged only for the same title and only if defective. NOOKs purchased from other retailers or sellers are returnable only to the retailer or seller from which they are purchased, pursuant to such retailer's or seller's return policy. Magazines, newspapers, eBooks, digital downloads, and used books are not returnable or exchangeable. Defective NOOKs may be exchanged at the store in accordance with the applicable warranty.

Returns or exchanges will not be permitted (i) after 14 days or without receipt or (ii) for product not carried by Barnes & Noble or Barnes & Noble.com.

Policy on receipt may appear in two sections.

Return Policy

With a sales receipt or Barnes & Noble.com packing slip, a full refund in the original form of payment will be issued from any Barnes & Noble Booksellers store for returns of undamaged NOOKs, new and unread books, and unopened and undamaged music CDs, DVDs, vinyl records, toys/games and audio books made within 14 days of purchase from a

1

What Is Common Sense Assessment?

> *"Teachers assess to test; educators assess to assist learning."*
> —Dave Carter (2001)

Before we begin our journey into the common sense of assessment and grading, take a moment to reflect on your own past experiences as a student or a parent of a student, or perhaps on the actions of a teacher you know.

1. Did you ever receive a grade in school that you felt was unfair? What happened? Why was it unfair?

2. If you were to relive that experience, how would you change what happened to be a more fair outcome?

Common Sense Assessment and Grading

In your first explanation, look to see if there was a lack of common sense in how and why you received that grade. In your second response stating how you would have changed what happened, how does common sense enter into this new scenario? Now that you have created a mindset of what you believe to be fair in assessment and grading and how common sense plays a major role, let's move into how we can best achieve a common sense assessment approach in your classroom.

When you see the word *assessment* in the title of this book, you may immediately think, "Oh, no. Not another book on testing! That sounds boring." Since a book *can* be judged by its cover, there are some key concepts in the title of this book that must be discussed before we delve into the teacher-friendly strategies that are based on common sense. More specifically, we will discuss the concepts of assessment and grading as well as the essential principles of differentiated instruction that are integrated into the practices described in this book. Defining these concepts will provide a common language for effectively implementing teacher-friendly, common sense assessment and grading strategies in your classroom.

First, let's take an in-depth look at some key concepts of differentiated instruction. Next, we will take a look at the definitions of assessment, evaluation, and grading.

What Is Differentiated Instruction?

Differentiated instruction occurs when the process of teaching and learning takes into account an individual student's readiness level, interests, and preferred modes of learning. Amy Benjamin (2003) says differentiated instruction is "a term that refers to a variety of classroom practices that allow for differences in students' learning styles, interests, prior knowledge, socialization needs, and comfort zones." Differentiation includes how a student shows proficiency of content standards. This is particularly important in the context of this book.

The following are the 5 Essential Elements of differentiated instruction. Elements #1, #2, and #5 are specifically targeted in this book as they illustrate the key role that assessment and grading play in a differentiated classroom environment.

Element #1: Know the curriculum.

Curriculum is defined here as district standards, state standards, and/or the Common Core State Standards. It is crucial that these standards are clear and aligned throughout the grade levels. It is this clear and aligned curriculum that lends itself to being differentiated. The teacher starts with the standard, then assesses, and finally differentiates based on the results of the assessment.

Element #2: Be an assessment expert.

Assessment is a process of three stages: pre-assessment, formative assessment (ongoing), and summative assessment (final). Assessments come in many forms, so it is crucial that the teacher understands all aspects of how to assess as well as ways to modify any of these assessment types in order to create learning pathways for each student.

Element #3: Utilize flexible grouping strategies.

The teacher decides when students will work as a class, when they will work alone, and when they will work in small groups. The teacher also decides when to group students together with similar or mixed learning profiles, when to spend time instructing small groups, and when to spend time in conversation with individual students.

Element #4: Create tasks that are respectful of each learner.

The majority of the time, student work is interesting, challenging, and infused with opportunities for critical thinking for all students. Learning modalities and time given to complete each task are important factors to consider here.

Element #5: Grade to show growth.

A student's grade should reflect that student's mastery of grade-level standards, objectives, or benchmarks. Students are measured against the standards, not other students. In turn, these grades are tracked and reported in a way that indicates students' growth and progress over time.

Know the Curriculum

Start with the standard, then assess. Make this your mantra whenever you plan your assessments. Before you can differentiate, assess, or grade, you must know the standards and grade-level expectations for the content area. The goal for every student is to strive for mastery of the content. You are accountable for creating opportunities for this to happen and for teaching in order for students to attain mastery of the grade-level standards; students are accountable for learning in order to attain mastery. Every assessment that follows your instruction simply becomes the measuring tool by which you can determine mastery of those standards. Start with the standard, then assess.

Ask yourself these very important questions: Do I have a clear understanding of *what* content standards I am accountable to teach for grade-level mastery? Am I clear, and are my students clear, about what is considered mastery? (*Note*: The term *proficient* may be used instead of *mastery*.) Either term defines the percentage of the content the student is held accountable for. This percentage (e.g., 80 percent, 90 percent, etc.) is usually pre-determined by the school or district. For consistency in this book, I will use the term *mastery*.

If you answered *No* to one or both of the questions above, then before you proceed, seek clarity first. You must know what you are supposed to teach and assess—meaning standards, not book chapters—and what is considered mastery in order for you to grade fairly and make decisions that will drive your instruction. Once you are clear on the content at your grade level, then you can proceed to strategies for assessing, measuring, and evaluating your students' progress toward mastery.

What Is Your Curriculum?

Is the curriculum your textbooks, programs, and kits? No! Is the curriculum your state standards, Common Core or otherwise? Yes! Textbooks, programs, and kits are resources and tools for teaching your grade-level standards. Your curriculum is your standards! Figure 1.1 is an Instruction and Assessment Model that shows a standards-focused, assessment-driven pathway for instruction.

Figure 1.1 Instruction and Assessment Model

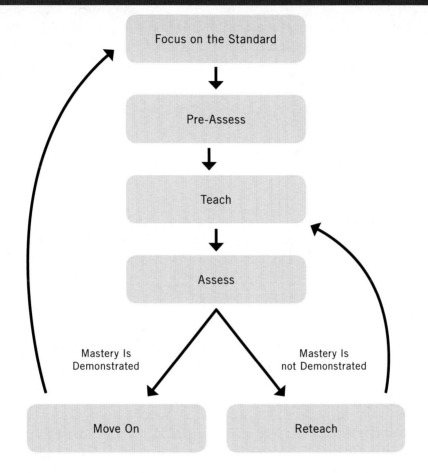

The focus is on the grade-level content standards and/or concepts. Start with the standard(s) in mind. Then, pre-assess, teach, and assess. Then, move on or reteach, if needed. After reteaching, assess again. Repeat this process for every standard or group of standards for every unit. This cycle will take students on a continuous journey up the assessment and evaluation learning curve toward mastery. Let's see how this looks in the classroom.

1. Focus on the standard

Mr. Johnson is ready to plan a unit on the Civil War. He chunks unit standards into manageable groups and time frames. The first standard is *Students will understand the causes of the Civil War.*

2. Pre-Assess

Mr. Johnson administers a "ticket-out" pre-assessment (described in Chapter 3) to see what students already know. Using this data, he then plans his instruction around what students need most. He has assessed what students already know and therefore where less time is needed in instruction.

3. Teach

Mr. Johnson instructs his students on this standard.

4. Assess

Mr. Johnson assesses for understanding and makes adjustments to his original lesson plan, using the assessment data. He asks: Is more instruction needed? Do I move forward with the whole class? Do I reteach those students who need it and allow others to move on?

5. Reteach

Mr. Johnson then reteaches if the results of the assessment reflect this need. After more instruction, he assesses for understanding once again.

6. Move On

When it is evident through assessment that gaps of understanding have closed to a reasonable degree (i.e., the majority of students understand at a level of mastery and the few remaining will get continual reinforcement as the next standard is applied), Mr. Johnson moves on to begin the cycle with a new standard or set of standards. The process is then repeated for every standard in that unit.

The standards that are currently being taught should be posted in a conspicuous place in the classroom for all eyes. Cognitive Theory Principles tell us that teachers must set a purpose and prime the brain for learning in order to make content relevant (Wormeli 2007). When the content is relevant, connections are made and, consequently, information is retained and understood. Conspicuous places might include the front of the room above the board, near the door where the students enter and leave, or in an area of the room where students engage in small-group instruction on a regular basis. Standards for the entire unit can take the form of a checklist that students keep in their portfolios. Standards currently being taught are checked. This is especially helpful because the students can see where they are in the "big picture" of the entire unit.

Be an Assessment Expert

In order to be an expert in anything, you must be a research junkie, gathering as much information about the topic as you possibly can. You're reading this book, aren't you? That's a great start! But don't stop here. Comb the Internet, drill the experts in your area, and attend workshops on assessment. Leave no stone unturned as you seek information about what assessment truly is and how you can apply it in your classroom. If you have engaged in vast and diverse research from many sources, apply that research to areas of need in your professional practice and continue to do so as new research emerges. Then, you can safely call yourself an expert. Just remember, even experts never stop their research and applications!

Grade to Show Growth

Grade books and reporting tools should be designed to show a starting and ending point of understanding during the course of instruction for each standard. Starting and ending points give the teacher a look at what the student knows or does not know and where instruction is needed in order to achieve mastery of the standard. (Inputting grades in a manner that will show progress over time provides a clear indication of how the student has moved forward on a continuum toward mastery.) Student growth rates vary. Some students will achieve mastery sooner than others, but all students will succeed to their highest potential when given the time they need. This individual progression through the standards should be reflected in the way that grades are tracked and reported.

What Defines Assessment, Evaluation, Grades, and Reporting?

The terms *assessment*, *evaluation*, *grade*, and *reporting* are often used interchangeably, but they do not mean the same thing. The terms will be used throughout the book, so it is important that their differences be clarified. I will go into more detail and give some examples of each one later in the chapter.

Assessment is the gathering and reviewing of data. Everything students say and do is a form of data that can be assessed.

Evaluation is the judgment of the data. This judgment can come in the form of check marks, grades, smiley faces, teachers' thoughts or observations (e.g., "It seems that John does not understand."), and more.

Grades are a form of evaluation or judgment. They can be points, letters, numbers, etc.

Reporting is the process of sharing grades with others, such as students, other teachers, administrators, and/or parents.

In our fast-paced classrooms, with all that we have to teach, we sometimes tend to teach, assess, and move on without considering the results of the assessment. Then, we do the same with the next concept: teach, assess, and move on. It's as though we expect that students have learned simply from taking the test as we move on to the next concept. Actually, the assessment is the collection of the data, and the evaluation of that data tells the teacher what to do next (i.e., either move on or reteach).

Assessment Should Improve Performance, Not Just Audit It!

You don't weigh a pig to fatten it. Rather, the pig is weighed (*assessment:* the pig weighs 75 pounds); the problem is diagnosed (*evaluation:* the pig is underweight); and then a prescription is filled (*data-driven strategy:* feed the pig). In the same way, assessment should always lead to diagnosis and prescription.

In the classroom, assessments do not help students learn content. The assessment is the measurement tool or, in the example, the pig scale. The results of the assessment inform the teacher about what needs to be done next. Either the teacher needs to provide further instruction or move on—feed the pig or leave him be! You may think this is a no-brainer concept. However, I have encountered situations in classrooms where if students did poorly on an assessment, they were merely given the assessment again and again until they "got it." Of course, they never did. The only result was frustration by the teacher and students and a tragic waste of everyone's precious time.

The Assessment and Evaluation Learning Curve

To avoid the pitfalls described, let's take a look at the nature of assessment and how it works. Have you ever said when you are in the process of learning something new that you were "on a learning curve?" That learning curve is a hill where you start from the bottom and work your way up to the top. As you near the top, the hill curves, crests, and finally plateaus. Picture Rocky Balboa running up that mountain of stairs as he prepares himself for his next fight. Hear the music in the background as he climbs: "Getting Strong Now!" He reaches the top with arms raised to the heavens. He turns, sees where he has been, and rejoices in his success at reaching the top. Learning curves are like that! Now, let's put students at the bottom of that stairway, only this is a stairway of knowledge. They struggle on the journey upward and rejoice when they reach the top.

Figure 1.2 is an Assessment and Evaluation Learning Curve. It shows assessment as a journey that begins at the bottom of a hill with pre-assessments, continues up through formative assessments, climbs over that final crest, and finishes at the uppermost plateau of summative assessments.

The assessment journey is an instructional model for the teacher, and it is a process for the students. It is a means to an end, and the end is mastery of content. You can use this curve to guide you through every unit and every standard that you teach.

Figure 1.2 Assessment and Evaluation Learning Curve

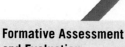

Summative Assessment and Evaluation

Final gathering and judgment of data

Assessment Examples:

Writing Samples

Pictures/Diagrams

Oral Presentations

Evaluation Examples:

Letter Grades

Points/Percentages

Rubrics

Formative Assessment and Evaluation

Gathering and judgment of data for diagnostic and prescription purposes

Assessment Examples:

Writing Samples

Pictures/Diagrams

Oral Presentations

Evaluation Examples:

Letter Grades

Points/Percents

Rubrics/Check Marks

Pre-Assessment and Evaluation

Gathering of data to see who the student is and what he or she already knows

Assessment Examples:

Inventories/Surveys

Writing Samples

Pictures/Diagrams

Oral Presentations

Evaluation Examples:

Mental Notes

Check Marks

Below are brief descriptions of what each "step" on the learning curve is all about. More detail will be shared in Chapters 2, 3, and 4, respectively.

Pre-Assessment

This is the time when the teacher gathers crucial information about the students for efficient and purposeful planning. In this step, the teacher decides which standards within the unit to emphasize, how much time to spend on each of those standards, and how to create specific learning pathways for students based on their learning modalities, interests, and readiness levels. Some examples of pre-assessments are shown in the diagram; more examples are offered in Chapter 2.

Formative Assessment

This step is sometimes referred to as *informative assessment*. Formative assessment is when students practice and the teacher reviews the practice assessments to see where to go with his or her instruction. Formative assessment must be followed with corrective instruction.

After formative assessment, feedback, and corrective instruction, students must have an opportunity to show the level of understanding they have now achieved. Some examples of formative assessments are shown in the diagram; more examples are offered in Chapter 3.

Summative Assessment

This is the time when students show final progress in relation to mastery of content. Evaluations for these assessments are noted for final reporting purposes. Some examples of summative assessments are shown in the diagram; more examples are offered in Chapter 4.

Recommendations for Pre-, Formative, and Summative Assessments

Here are two recommendations for assessments:

1. Inform students of the concepts and skills necessary for achievement and the criteria that will be used to judge achievement.

2. Give students more than one opportunity to show their new level of understanding of content (Marzano 2000). Be sure students are given enough opportunities to show their level of understanding of content in a variety of ways that align with their learning modalities.

Why Some Succeed and Others Do Not

As I pointed out in the second recommendation, not only must students be given more than one opportunity to show new levels of understanding, but they must also be given more than one way to show this. Often, teachers give tests and quizzes, which all require written, drawn, or fill-in-the-blank responses. This works for some students, but others may struggle with their writing or drawing skills. They may know the content but have a difficult time with the mode of the assessment.

Choices Given

Consider your students' learning modalities (see Chapter 2, which discusses multiple intelligences and learning styles). Keep those modalities in mind, and whenever possible, give students choices for how they want to show what they know so that you can have a more accurate measurement of what they know about the content. The format of the assessment can skew the picture of what the student knows if the format is not a good match with his or her learning modalities. For example, students could be asked to write a short essay on one assessment and then perhaps the next attempt could be through diagramming or role-playing.

Time Given

Consider the fact that students process information at different rates. Give each student the time he or she needs to complete activities and products. This can be done by making sure you are not giving students too much work to accomplish in the amount of time they have. Or allow students who need more time to finish the assessment later, either in another classroom, during the next class, at home, or at any other time that is agreed upon by you and the student.

Assessments and Evaluations Can Take On Many Forms

All assessments must be followed by evaluation whether it is a mental judgment made on your part, a check mark on the product, or a letter grade. If you are not judging each assessment, then why are you giving it? All assessments inform instruction. Students figure out right away that if the work they complete is not judged, then it must be busywork and therefore not important. If you do not have time to evaluate or grade the assignments you give, only administer assessments that you have time to evaluate with a discerning eye.

Assessments and evaluations can take on many different forms. Pre-assessments, formative assessments, and summative assessments do not always have to be paper-pencil format. Evaluations don't always have to be grades. First, let's consider the different ways in which students can show what they know.

Assessment Types

There are many different types of assessments. This list offers some suggestions:

- dramatic presentations
- surveys
- graphic organizers
- checklists
- oral reports
- student-directed mini-lessons
- written documents
- projects
- tests
- songs
- quizzes

Evaluation Types

There are many different ways to evaluate student learning. This list offers some suggestions:

- rubric scores
- graphs
- letter grades
- check marks
- percentage scores
- symbols
- pictures

It's not the modality of the assessment that determines if it is a pre-assessment, a formative assessment, or a summative assessment. It's *when* the assessment is given that determines this.

Now, let's continue the journey to discovering hands-on, teacher-friendly assessment and grading strategies that you can implement immediately in your differentiated classroom. That journey begins in the next chapter with pre-assessments.

Review and Reflect

1. How do you differentiate assessments to meet your students' needs?

2. Do you have a clear understanding of what the content standards are for your grade level? If so, how do you determine whether your students have mastered those standards?

3. Look at the highlighted 5 Essential Elements of differentiated instruction. Which element do you think is most important as it relates to assessment and grading? Why? Does the way you assess and grade your students reflect this principle?

2

Pre-Assessments

"You must train the children to their studies in a playful manner and without any air of constraint with the further object of discerning more readily the natural bent of their respective characters."

—Plato

Know Your Students: What Needs to Be Assessed?

Several years ago, when I first heard the term *differentiated instruction*, I thought, "Oh, that is just a new name for what I've been doing in my classroom for years!" I always had a student-centered environment where I used best practices on a daily basis. I attended every workshop and conference that came along to learn more about how to teach to students' learning styles.

I had been using the multiple intelligences approach to teaching based on Howard Gardner's work (1999) before this study ever came along! Sometimes I had my students writing on chart paper, drawing, writing, working in cooperative groups, learning to music, moving around the room, or sitting on the floor. Sometimes they were noisy. Sometimes they were quiet. So what was so different about this new differentiated instruction? "Nothing," I thought.

I thought wrong. As I learned more about differentiated instruction, I realized that, yes, I was teaching to different learning profiles. I was using best practices. But I was not differentiating instruction. I was using what I learned about best practices in a whole group. When I had students write, all of them were writing. When I had them learn to music, all of them were learning to music. When I had them do projects, write on chart paper, paint, draw, be noisy, or be quiet, all of them were doing those things. I used best practices in my classroom as a whole group. If you are doing these things, don't stop! Teaching as a whole group is a good thing, now and then. But just know that when students are doing the same thing at the same time in the same way, you may be using best practices, but you are not differentiating.

Differentiated instruction is defined as a "variety of classroom practices that allow for differences in students' learning styles, interests, prior knowledge, socialization needs, and comfort zones" (Benjamin 2003). So how can we know the individual learning needs, styles, and interests of our students? Through assessment!

Differentiating instruction is when you find out key information (which will be described later in this chapter) about each student and then use that information to create personalized pathways for learning. You should plan your instruction based on this data. The results make for a whole new look in your differentiated classroom, different from what I had been doing previously. At any given time, some students may be drawing while some may be writing. Some may be learning to music while some are not. Some may be grouped while some may be working individually.

In order to differentiate instruction in your classroom, you must gather data about your students. This should be done at the beginning of the school year so that you can start differentiating your instruction right away. There are three major areas that need to be pre-assessed in order to truly know your students and effectively create customized learning pathways through the curriculum. These areas are:

- Learning Modalities
- Interests
- Readiness for Content

Principals and teachers often ask me, "What is not negotiable when it comes to first steps in implementing differentiated instruction in your classroom?" My response is, "Pre-assessing your students." If you don't know how the students learn, what their interests are, and what their readiness for content is, then how can you create learning pathways for individuals or groups of students? Without this information, teachers have no option but to go back to teaching as a whole group: the same thing at the same time in the same way.

Differentiated instruction is rooted in assessment. In order to design instruction and assessments that will continually give you an accurate picture of what students need, you must first find out who your students are and what they are capable of.

Learning Modalities

Let's start with gathering data about students' learning modalities. Under the umbrella of learning modalities, the terms *learning styles* and *multiple intelligences* have emerged and have been used interchangeably. Indeed, both terms suggest that students have different approaches to learning. For the purposes of this book, however, I will refer to *learning styles* and *multiple intelligences* as separate concepts with unique definitions.

Learning Styles

Learning styles are defined as modalities that are influenced by personality and environment. They are learned behaviors. Joseph Pear (2001), a learning-styles theorist, defines learning as "a dependency of current behavior on the environment as a function of prior interaction between sensory-motor activity and the environment." Examples from Richard Felder and Barbara Soloman include active learners, reflective learners, intuitive learners, verbal learners, and global learners (Soloman and Felder 1999).

Learning style inventories and surveys are readily available online by searching *learning style inventories.*

Multiple Intelligences

The Multiple Intelligences Theory is based on the work of Howard Gardner (1983). Gardner takes a more physiological approach to how we learn. The theory says that the cellular make up of the brain determines our strengths and how we learn best. Gardner defined eight different intelligence categories, which are teacher friendly and easy to implement in the classroom.

Figure 2.1 is an overview of the multiple intelligences. These descriptions can help you understand your students' strengths and in turn help you to create appropriate assessments for your diverse learners.

Figure 2.1 Multiple Intelligences Descriptions

Logical/Mathematical

Person excels with logic, abstractions, reasoning, and numbers.

Verbal/Linguistic

Person displays a facility with words and languages.

Visual/Spatial

Person is aware of physical space and enjoys using models, graphics, charts, and drawings.

Musical/Rhythmical

Person is sensitive to sounds, rhythms, tones, and music.

Bodily/Kinesthetic

Person possesses control of his or her bodily motions and can handle objects skillfully.

Naturalist/Environmental

Person is nurturing, relates information to natural surroundings, and is sensitive to his or her five senses.

Interpersonal

Person communicates effectively and empathizes easily with others; an extrovert.

Intrapersonal

Person is introspective, self-reflective, intuitive, and typically introverted.

Planning instruction based on the multiple intelligences is an integral part of differentiated instruction as this theory lends itself to different product choices and grouping configurations for the diverse learners in the classroom. This can mean creating instruction or assignments based on intelligence strengths. It can also mean purposeful grouping of students based on their intelligence strengths, either homogeneously with students of the same intelligence strengths or heterogeneously with a mix of intelligence strengths in order to maximize learning.

Learning styles and multiple intelligences theory integrate nicely together. Think of brain-based learning as the umbrella that presides over environmental-based learning. The two work together as learners grow and interact with their environment. For example, you may have a student (we will call her Judy) who is strong in the logical/mathematical intelligence and is also a competitive learner. To optimize Judy's learning, you will want to create assessments that allow her to work out solutions in her head before writing them down or verbalizing them. This addresses her logical/mathematical intelligence strength. Judy will want to keep a running chart of scores for each assessment so that she competes against herself to do better every time.

Both approaches to learning modalities—environmental and physiological—can work together in order to provide teachers with opportunities to collect data and create effective learning pathways for students.

Through my work with teachers around the country, I have found that most of them know of the multiple intelligences theory. Some of them implement it in their classrooms. But very few actually diagnose their students' intelligences. In order to create pathways to content understanding for every student, you must know how their brains learn. It is important to administer these inventories, preferably at the beginning of the year, so that you can use the data to drive instruction and to create assessments that will give accurate information about what students have learned. One idea, if you are in a departmentalized setting, is to designate one classroom where the teacher will administer the inventory to the students and then share the results with the other teachers.

Multiple Intelligences Diagnostic Tool 1 and *Multiple Intelligences Diagnostic Tool 2* are based on the Multiple Intelligences Theory (Gardner 1983). Intelligence Inventories are included in Appendix A for grades K–2, 3–8, 9–12.

Multiple Intelligences Diagnostic Tool 1

Grade Levels

K–2

Materials

- *How Are You Smart?* (Appendix A)

- Sets of eight crayons (yellow, blue, red, orange, green, purple, black, pink)

- *Multiple Intelligences Behavior Inventory Grades K–2* (Appendix A)

Procedure

Note: You should meet with a small group of no more than four students at a location separate from the rest of the class. This activity can be done during center time or individual project time by you or by a paraprofessional. Each session should take about thirty minutes. Work with as many groups in one day as time allows.

1. Provide students with instructions for writing their names, the date, and for coloring in the circles on the chart. For example, "Write your name on the top of the chart." (Wait for students to do so.) "Write today's date." (Wait for students to do so.) "Color the circles with the colors at the bottom of the chart." (Walk them through each color.) "Now, set these charts aside for just a few minutes."

How Are You Smart?

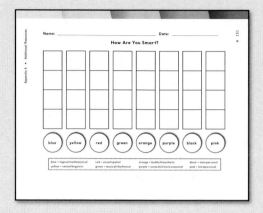

2. Begin with dialogue about differences. For example:

"What are your names?" (Let students respond.)

"We all have different names! I'll bet there are lots of things about us that are different."

"Li, what's your favorite flavor of ice cream?"

"Carmen, what's your favorite flavor?"

"Is Li smarter than Carmen because he likes chocolate and she likes strawberry?" (Let students respond.)

"Is Becky smarter than Samir because she likes vanilla and he likes chocolate chip?" (Let students respond.)

3. Continue asking about differences. For example:

"Becky, what is your favorite thing to do when you get home from school?"

"Samir, what is your favorite thing to do when you get home from school?"

"Is Samir smarter than Becky because he likes to watch TV and she likes to play with her dog?" (Let students respond.)

"Is Carmen smarter than Li because she likes to play outside and he likes to play in his room?" (Let students respond.)

4. Continue the dialogue about how it is nice that we are all different. For example:

"What would the world be like if everyone was the same? What would the grocery store look like if everyone liked the same kinds of food? It would be pretty boring!"

Then, tell students that you are going to read some statements, and you will tell them something about each one. If they agree that the statement is something they like or something they are good at, then they should pick up the crayon that matches the description and fill in one square for that color. Students should not pick up the crayon until they have decided if the statement is what they like or what they are good at.

Say to students, "When we're finished, we'll see how different we are from one another! Okay, let's begin!"

5. Read from the *Multiple Intelligences Behavior Inventory Grades K–2* (Appendix A). Read one statement at a time. Mix them up. Read one statement from verbal, then one from musical, then one from kinesthetic, until you have read them all. Tell students to fill in one square with the appropriate color if the sentence describes them.

Multiple Intelligences Behavior Inventory Grades K–2

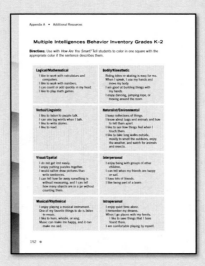

6. After you read a statement, be sure that you give the students the option to color the square or to not color the square. Primary students have the tendency to color the squares regardless of their likes or dislikes. They need to be reminded of their options. Commend them continually for being honest in their answers.

7. Intermittently throughout the session, interject this reminder: "Wow, look at that! Some of us like (insert object/activity) and some of us don't! That's because we are all different!" Have students say the word *different* aloud as you say it.

8. When the session is over, have students show their papers to show one another. Remark how everyone is different and that makes us each very special.

9. Post the completed charts on a bulletin board in a colorful display as a reminder to students and to you about how they each think and learn.

Multiple Intelligences Diagnostic Tool 2

Grade Levels

3–12

Materials

- *Which Intelligence Are You?* (Appendix A)
- Sets of colored markers in assorted bright colors
- *Multiple Intelligences Behavior Inventory Grades 3–8* or *Multiple Intelligences Behavior Inventory Grades 9–12* (Appendix A)

Procedures

Note: Whether the *Multiple Intelligences Behavior Inventory Grades 3–8* or the *Multiple Intelligences Behavior Inventory Grades 9–12* is used, students complete the same graph.

1. Spend time teaching students about the intelligences before administering the diagnostic survey. Facilitate discussions about what the intelligences are and that intelligence strengths are hereditary. Explain that we tend to engage in activities that reflect our intelligences and eventually choose our careers based on these strengths. Involve students in hands-on activities. For example, have students cut out pictures in magazines and make collages depicting each of the intelligences.

2. Distribute copies of *Which Intelligence Are You?* Explain to students that you will read aloud a description. Students could read it on their own, but reading each intelligence scenario aloud with them allows you to interject information or examples as you go. Also, explain that once each description is read aloud, they will mark the graph in response to each intelligence scenario: 10 is *most like me* and 1 is *least like me*.

Which Intelligence Are You?

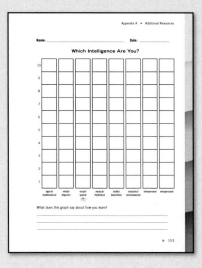

3. Read aloud each description and have students mark their graphs accordingly. You may choose to complete the survey along with students. They enjoy this, and it may give you insight into which intelligences you've been teaching to and how to "change things up" to strike a balance.

Multiple Intelligences Behavior Inventory Grades 3–8

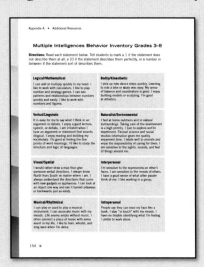

Multiple Intelligences Behavior Inventory Grades 9–12

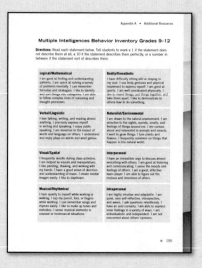

4. After students mark all bars on the graph, have them color the bars with bright colors. The use of colors depicts a "celebration" of their strengths and how they learn best. Display the graphs in a conspicuous place in the classroom. You, each student, and the rest of the class should use this data throughout the year to help with teaching, grouping, and peer tutoring.

Observation Checklist

Figure 2.2 shows an observation checklist that requires nothing of the students but for them to behave naturally as they interact with their surroundings. Use this along with the preceding inventories to assess students—you can never gather too much data!

This checklist works with any grade level. Here's how it works:

1. Write students' names in the column on the left. You will probably need to use multiple sheets, depending on the number of students you will be observing.

2. Make a tally in the appropriate box for each student when you see him or her exhibit the behavior described in the intelligences boxes. This need not be contrived—simply make those marks whenever the behavior is observed.

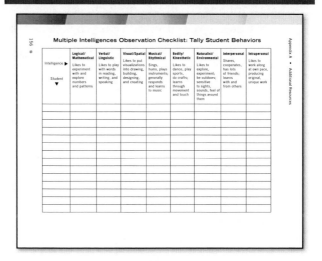

Figure 2.2 Multiple Intelligences Observation Checklist: Tally Student Behaviors

3. As the marks begin to accumulate, see where they occur most frequently for each student. The totals will give you information on the intelligence strengths of your students. This resource can be found in Appendix A.

Interests

Have you ever found yourself exclaiming in despair, "I just can't motivate this student!" Let me reassure you that sometimes a person just cannot be motivated by anyone. Motivation is a personal decision that comes from within one's self. For example, you can't motivate someone to quit smoking. You can't motivate someone to lose weight. You can't motivate someone to be happy. You can't motivate them, but you can get their attention! Once you have their attention, then whatever you used to get their attention can be motivating for them. How can you get your students' attention? Find out where their interests lie and integrate these things into their studies.

For example, let's say you're trying to teach Christopher how to write complete sentences. He has a hard time transfering his thoughts to paper. You know that he's interested in action heroes, so you have him fill in the balloons of an action-hero comic strip, using complete sentences. You caught his attention and now Christopher is motivated to write.

Survey your students' interests, and use this information to guide your instruction. Interest surveys can be found online by conducting simple web searches. Also involve the parents. Have you ever had this conversation with parents during conference time? Teacher: "Marvin is such a good role model for following class rules and is always eager to help others." Parent: "Are we talking about the same child? He is so opposite of that at home!" What you know about the student and what the parent knows can be quite different! Survey the parents, too.

Figures 2.3, 2.4, and 2.5 are interest surveys, one for younger students, older students, and parents. They have been adapted from a study by Joan Franklin Smutny (1997). Have students

Figure 2.3 About Me! (For Younger Students)

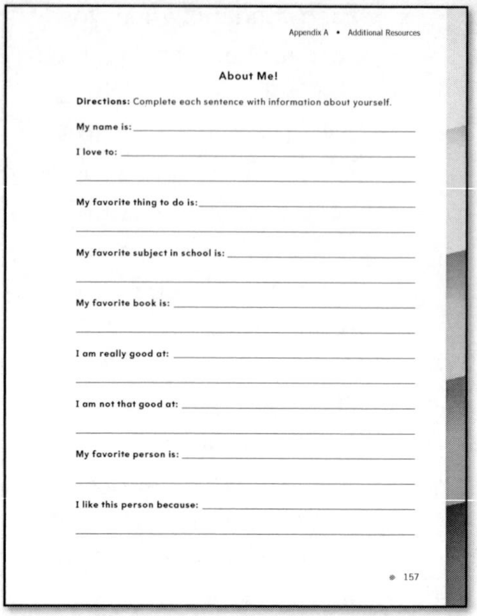
Appendix A • Additional Resources

About Me!

Directions: Complete each sentence with information about yourself.

My name is: ____

I love to: ____

My favorite thing to do is: ____

My favorite subject in school is: ____

My favorite book is: ____

I am really good at: ____

I am not that good at: ____

My favorite person is: ____

I like this person because: ____

157

Figure 2.4 About Me! (For Older Students)

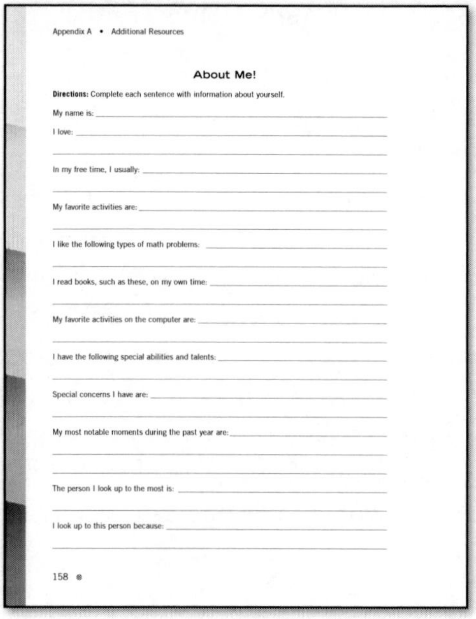
Appendix A • Additional Resources

About Me!

Directions: Complete each sentence with information about yourself.

My name is: ____

I love: ____

In my free time, I usually: ____

My favorite activities are: ____

I like the following types of math problems: ____

I read books, such as these, on my own time: ____

My favorite activities on the computer are: ____

I have the following special abilities and talents: ____

Special concerns I have are: ____

My most notable moments during the past year are: ____

The person I look up to the most is: ____

I look up to this person because: ____

158

complete the *About Me!* survey that is appropriate for their grade level. The survey can be given in class or at home; however, I recommend that they be completed at home. Students' responses may be more honest in the absence of peer influence. Choose the version of the survey that is most developmentally appropriate for your students. Send the parent survey home and have parents return it in a timely manner. Parents can complete it out themselves or together with their child. These resources can be found in Appendix A.

Figure 2.5 About My Child (For Parents)

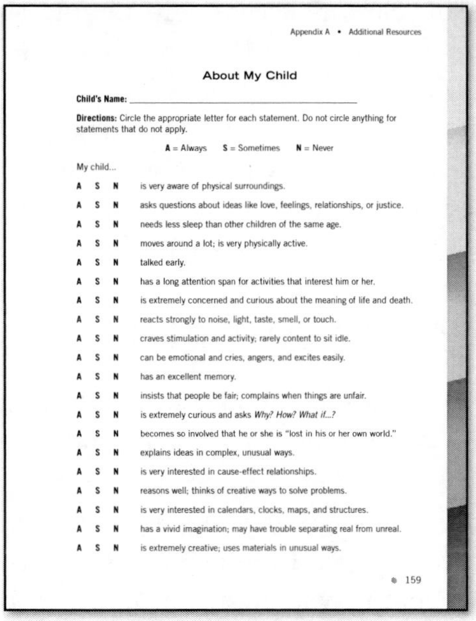
Appendix A • Additional Resources

About My Child

Child's Name: ______________________

Directions: Circle the appropriate letter for each statement. Do not circle anything for statements that do not apply.

A = Always **S** = Sometimes **N** = Never

My child...

A S N is very aware of physical surroundings.
A S N asks questions about ideas like love, feelings, relationships, or justice.
A S N needs less sleep than other children of the same age.
A S N moves around a lot; is very physically active.
A S N talked early.
A S N has a long attention span for activities that interest him or her.
A S N is extremely concerned and curious about the meaning of life and death.
A S N reacts strongly to noise, light, taste, smell, or touch.
A S N craves stimulation and activity; rarely content to sit idle.
A S N can be emotional and cries, angers, and excites easily.
A S N has an excellent memory.
A S N insists that people be fair; complains when things are unfair.
A S N is extremely curious and asks *Why? How? What if...?*
A S N becomes so involved that he or she is "lost in his or her own world."
A S N explains ideas in complex, unusual ways.
A S N is very interested in cause-effect relationships.
A S N reasons well; thinks of creative ways to solve problems.
A S N is very interested in calendars, clocks, maps, and structures.
A S N has a vivid imagination; may have trouble separating real from unreal.
A S N is extremely creative; uses materials in unusual ways.

159

Readiness for Content

This last type of pre-assessment is the most widely used. You have probably pre-assessed your students now and then before starting a unit of study. The intent here is to find out what students know or don't know about a topic you are about to cover. Once you find out, be sure that you use this information to drive your instruction. Sometimes, teachers pre-assess for prior knowledge yet still cover the entire unit, leaving nothing out and spending the same amount of time on a topic as it appears in the materials. It brings up this question: Why pre-assess if you're going to teach it all anyway?

In an article that discusses school reform and classroom practice, Larry Cuban (2011) addresses how today's teachers use assessments to drive future instruction. He claims that "Teachers' informal assessments of students... would lead to altered lessons. Analysis of annual test results that showed patterns in student errors helped teachers figure out better sequencing of content and different ways to teach particular topics."

As teachers, we want to pre-assess for content knowledge in order to drive our instruction. By finding out what students know or don't know, you can plan your unit accordingly. Let me ask you this: Do you have so much extra time in your day that you find yourself killing time? I thought not! So it makes sense to find out what students already know about a topic, then plan accordingly. A lack of time is a huge issue for teachers, and since every minute of the school day is precious, spend that time wisely. Start out by spending less time on what students already know and more time on what they don't. Content pre-assessments will give you this information. As a result of these pre-assessments, you may decide to spend *no* time on areas where students showed mastery of the content.

Here is an example of the use of pre-assessment from my own classroom. I was preparing to teach a standard included in an earth science unit. The standard read, "Students will understand differences between and the formation of stalagmites and stalactites." Before planning the lessons around this standard, I pre-assessed students by asking them to describe what they thought they knew about the two formations. I asked them questions, such as *What are they? How are they formed? Where can you find them?* I did not give the names of the formations; I simply provided pictures for them to reference. In reviewing their completed pre-assessments, I discovered that almost all of my students had a good understanding of what the formations were, their differences, and how they are formed. Based on this data, I decided not to spend a lot of time on definitions and processes but to go right into application-based activities. Their pre-assessments also raised a "red flag" for me, informing me that I needed to add these terms to the students' spelling list. The reason was that almost every student spelled *stalagmites* correctly but spelled the other formations as *stalagtites*. I did spend my valuable time on this important lesson in spelling and how to remember that they are spelled differently from one another. I helped the students by using a memory aide. *Stalactites form from the ceiling down, so they are spelled with a* c *for* ceiling. *Stalagmites build from the ground up, so think* g *for* ground. I put the time into this standard where it was needed based on the data I received from students' pre-assessments.

If you have pre-assessed for content only periodically, you may eventually decide that it is worth your time to pre-assess before starting every unit. This way, you can hone your teaching time to concepts and standards that your students actually need instruction in. You are not wasting your time or the students' time on content they already know. Use pre-assessments to drive future instruction. In other words, you do have time to pre-assess, as it is this up-front investment that will save you time in the long run. You are spending more time on acceleration and less time on remediation.

In Chapter 1, various forms of assessments (including pre-assessments) were listed. On the following pages are specific examples that can be used for pre-assessment. Remember that anything a student says (e.g., verbal answers to questions or comments made while working on an assignment), does (e.g., role-playing, knitted brow, nervous behavior during an assessment, glassy-eyed bored expressions, finishing work early with high accuracy of content, finishing work late with low accuracy of content, or not turning in work), or creates (e.g., pictures, diagrams, essays, short-answer paragraphs, projects, or models) can be used as pre-assessment tools.

Here are samples of pre-assessments you can use for determining content understanding:

- "Hands-On" Research Visual Organizer
- Ticket In Pre-Assessment
- Anticipation Guide
- Concept Mind Map
- End-of-the-Unit Test

These samples can also be used as formative and summative assessments. Just about any assessment type can be used in all three categories (pre-, formative, and summative). It is not *the form* that determines the assessment type. It is *when* it is administered that makes that determination.

"Hands-On" Research Visual Organizer

You can use this visual organizer as a means of pre-assessment for a new unit study. Here are the steps needed to administer this pre-assessment:

1. Select a standards-based topic of study.

2. Have each student trace his or her hands on a plain sheet of paper.

3. Individually or with partners, have students write five things they already know about the topic on the fingers of one of their traced hands.

4. On the fingers of the other traced hand, have students write five questions that they would like to find answers to regarding the topic of study.

5. During the course of the unit, have students research to find the answers to their questions. These questions can also serve as guidelines for you as to what should be covered during the unit.

Ticket In Pre-Assessment

You can use the *Ticket In Pre-Assessment* at the beginning of a new unit (see Figure 2.6 and Appendix A). Introduce the topic to students. Then, assign this pre-assessment. The idea behind this strategy is that students would complete the assessment as homework and use it as their ticket in the door the following day. However, you should use the *Ticket In Pre-Assessment* flexibly in a manner that fits your class and schedule.

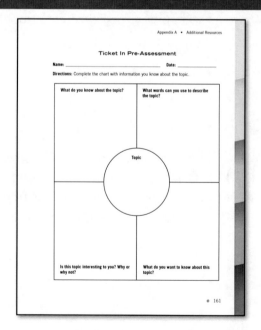

Figure 2.6 Ticket In Pre-Assessment

Anticipation Guide

With this strategy, you provide students with general statements related to the topic they are going to learn about and ask them to determine if the statements are true or false.

The *Anticipation Guide* provides a connection to prior knowledge, engages students with the topic, and encourages them to explore their own thoughts and opinions. See Figure 2.7. This resource can be found in Appendix A.

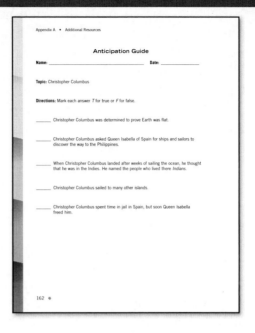

Figure 2.7 Anticipation Guide

Concept Mind Map

The *Concept Mind Map* is a graphic organizer that allows students to brainstorm ideas about a topic and define its characteristics. The concept, which can be an entire unit title or an individual standard, is written or drawn in the center oval. Students respond accordingly in each of the quadrants, either with words or pictures. See Figure 2.8. This resource can also be found in Appendix A.

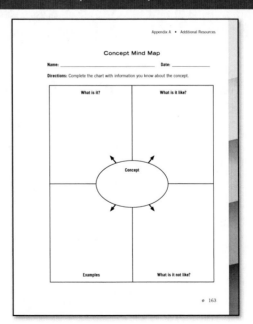

Figure 2.8 Concept Mind Map

End-of-the-Unit Test

Another way to pre-assess students for content is to give them the comprehensive summative test or chapter test at the *beginning* of the unit. After administering the test, review the answers immediately with the class. Have students check their own test by highlighting incorrect answers with highlighters. This can be a powerful opportunity for instruction as students can then correct any incorrect answers. By correcting the items they missed, they can preview upcoming concepts. This plants seeds in their brains as hooks for future learning. You are providing them with prior knowledge.

I have heard some teachers exclaim, "I'm not giving them the end-of-the-unit test, and especially not the answers! They will remember those answers when it comes time to give the test again and just write them down! That's cheating!" Isn't remembering the content the point? If my students can remember those answers after weeks of study, then I've done my job! And by giving them the comprehensive test before you actually teach the unit, you are exercising one of the cognitive theory principles, which states, "If information is to be learned, it must first be recognized as important. The more attention effectively directed toward what is to be learned, the higher the probability of learning" (DiPietro 1995). Using an end-of-the-unit test as a pre-assessment tool can be a powerful way to help students recognize the unit's most important concepts. After all, these concepts are, presumably, what they will be held accountable for in all end-of-the-unit assessments.

Evaluating Content Pre-Assessments

All assessments need to be evaluated for the purpose of planning and driving instruction, and pre-assessments are no exception. As mentioned in Chapter 1, evaluation is not synonymous with grading. Assessment is the gathering of data. Evaluation is the judgment of the data, and both come in many forms. A grade is only one form of evaluation, and this form may be used among others when judging formative and summative assessments. When evaluating pre-assessments, grades should not be used. Instead, use check marks, symbols like a smiley face, or fractions (e.g., three out of five correct), in order to highlight areas where instruction is needed. These types of evaluations lend themselves to prescriptive instruction rather than final judgments.

Once you have gathered the data and evaluated it, what do you do with the information? Use it to plan your lessons. Use it to drive your instruction from the first day of instruction. Formative assessments will be used to continue this process, but for now, use the pre-assessments to determine how you will approach the standards for the unit.

Figure 2.9 shows a *Prescription for Differentiation* graphic organizer that will help you to organize pre-assessment data into four categories: learning styles, multiple intelligences, interests, and readiness for content. If you have chosen not to assess in one of these four areas, simply leave it blank. This graphic organizer is intended to be used for diagnostic and prescriptive purposes. It should help you when you reflect on students' areas of need and how you can meet those needs.

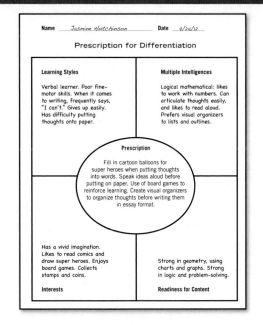

Figure 2.9 Sample Prescription for Differentiation

To use the graphic organizer, summarize the results of surveys and pre-assessments in the appropriate quadrants. Using the information from these quadrants, write a general prescription for differentiating instruction in the center circle. This prescription is used as a guide for creating learning pathways for that student for future instruction. In a nutshell, if you are using this data when planning your lessons, you are differentiating instruction! A blank template of this graphic organizer can be found in Appendix A.

Organizing the Data to Plan Instruction

Eventually, you want each student to fill out one *Prescription for Differentiation* sheet. Start with students in your class who stand out as having a greater need for immediate differentiation. All students have this need, but start with extremes for the sake of budgeting your time. Begin with the bored, struggling student, and/or the unmotivated student.

What I found most useful about having one sheet filled out for each student was that during my lesson planning when I needed to group students, I could shuffle the papers and "pile" those students into those groups according to any of the four quadrants. For example, if I needed to group by interests, I would make a pile of the students who had similar interests. The piles, of course, simulated the groups. Or if I needed to group students by readiness for content, I would create as many piles as I needed for homogeneous or heterogeneous grouping according to the information in that quadrant. The same went for grouping by learning styles and multiple intelligences.

We've pre-assessed students in four areas, we've evaluated, we've documented, and we've created prescriptions for academic success. Now we're ready to take that next step in assessment: formative assessment. In the eyes of tradition, this is a big and sometimes controversial step.

Review and Reflect

1. How do you pre-assess your students to find out their interests, learning modalities, multiple intellgiences, and readiness for content? Which strategies work best for you and why?

2. How do you use the data from your pre-assessments to plan lessons?

3. Which is the most important type of information you can gather from students for planning instruction to meet their needs: interests, learning modalities, multiple intelligences, or readiness for content? Why do you think so?

3

Formative Assessments

"Measurements are not to provide numbers but insight."
—Ingrid Bucher (1987)

This is the longest chapter in this book because formative assessment is at the heart and soul of the assessment cycle. This is when quality teaching must happen, when the "rubber meets the road." In other words, this is the crucial time when students are telling you what they need and when you are making decisions to adjust your teaching to meet those needs. This is when students are moving up the learning curve toward the ultimate goal, mastery of the content.

What Are Formative Assessments?

Formative assessment begins as soon as pre-assessment ends and instruction begins. Formative assessments come in many forms, including how students behave, and what they say, write, draw, build, and create. Indeed, as Carol Ann Tomlinson states, "I began to sense that virtually all student products and interactions can serve as informative assessment because I, as a teacher, have the power to use them that way" (2007). Formative assessment begins on the first day of instruction and continues every day in many forms. It is the "guided practice" in Madeline Hunter's model for planning instruction (1994): "Provide guided practice following instruction by having students answer questions, discuss with one another, demonstrate skills, or solve problems. Give immediate feedback and reteach if necessary." Formative assessments are used for diagnostic and prescriptive purposes. They provide the teacher with a compass that will determine what direction must be taken for future instruction. Substitute the word *formative* with *informative*, and that gives a good picture of the purpose of formative assessment: *informing* future instruction.

Since formative assessments are considered practice for students and are meant to provide the teacher with information on student progress, they should not be included in the mix for final reporting on a report card. Students need ample time to practice new concepts or skills. As Robert Marzano states, "Students need more than one opportunity to show their new level of understanding" (2000). Students must know that they are allowed to make mistakes as they are learning something new.

Traditionally, all assessments are graded and included in the report card. In this case, when students make mistakes, there is no room for students to improve that grade before it hits the grade book and, ultimately, the report card. Students need to trust that they will not be penalized for taking the time they need. Oftentimes teachers understandably believe that if they don't assign a grade that ends up on the report card, students will not take the assessment seriously. Please understand that I am not saying that formative assessments are not evaluated or graded. Students must know that these assessments will be evaluated and that they will be held accountable for those formative assessments.

One way you can get that message across to students is by using checklists. Checklists make great accountability tools. All assignments given during the formative assessment period can be put on a checklist to indicate whether that the assignment has been completed. These checklists may also hold the respective evaluation for those assignments. If there is a box left unchecked, students are subject to consequences for incomplete work. The consequences may involve parent conferencing, working on the assignment during other points in the day, or whatever consequence you deem appropriate. But giving a lower grade on a report card must not be the consequence in this case, in light of the fact that formative assessment evaluations are not included in the mix on a report card. Students need to know that although formative assessment scores do not make it to the report card, they will still be held accountable for getting the work done. It's also appropriate for students to know that these assessments will be used for giving you information about how students are progressing toward understanding the content and that this information will drive future instruction.

Carol Ann Tomlinson, in her 2007 article "Learning to Love Assessment," states, "About the same time that understanding…emerged in my thinking, I began to sense that filling a grade book was both less interesting and less useful than trying to figure out what individual students knew, understood, or could do."

Once students have been given time to practice new skills on their journey to the top of the learning curve, the assessment mode then switches to summative. The summative assessments are what is reported on the final reporting tool. I will discuss this in depth in Chapter 4.

This common-sense perspective on formative assessments as practice is best illustrated through the following analogies. In football, the players don't practice just once and then play the opposing teams in competitive games. There are many practices that precede those games, during which the coach assesses each player on every move, every play, and every strategy. Based on these assessments, the coach diagnoses and prescribes what he or she thinks will help the players improve their skills. After many practices, once the coach sees consistency in the mastery of the moves and strategies, he or she then decides it's time for the players to play the scheduled games in the competitive arena. The practices are formative (diagnostic/prescriptive). The games are summative (final shows of mastery).

The same can be said when someone learns to play a musical instrument. The student is taught how to play the instrument and commences to practice. When the music teacher's evaluation of these practices indicates that the student is ready to perform, the mode switches to summative, which may be playing for audiences in the concert arena. The public did not see the practices, but the end results ensured that there was indeed adequate practice time! The practices are formative. The concerts are summative.

I understand the frustration you may possibly be feeling from these anologies. You may feel that you don't have the freedom to change what and how assessments are recorded and reported. Perhaps you are working with a grade book or a reporting system that has been chosen by your district or school, and this system is mandated. Perhaps this system may not be consistent with the notion of excluding formative assessments in the mix for final reporting. My recommendation, in this case, is to look closely at your current system. Often, the grade book and/or report card can be modified. Look to see if the system you use offers the option to select only those assessments that will be included in the final report card. If not, do what you can within the parameters you must follow to allow final grades to reflect summative, more so than formative, assessment.

Maybe you are feeling as if you don't have the power to change how assessments are entered and reported. After all, a school system is a large body that must take a consistent approach to assessment. Maybe you feel as if you are on the bottom when it comes to decision-making. I get that. However, change has to start somewhere, and it often begins with (in this case) a report card committee made up of teachers whose job is to research and recommend more effective grading and reporting systems. Or it may take a faculty study of a book like this one, a professional development conference, or a guest speaker on the subject to start the conversation and open minds to a better way.

In any case, do what you can to practice this common-sense approach to assessment within your present circumstances. There is a reason why you picked up this book. Perhaps the reason is that you see a need for change. Change starts with you. Try one thing today, then another later on. Start with baby steps. Then find your stride!

Planning Activities for Formative Assessments

Use the following criteria to plan formative assessment activities that will show what students know and can do. (*Note:* The same criteria can also apply when planning for summative assessments.)

Criteria #1: Assessments are natural, not contrived. The activities are integrated within the lesson, not added on.

Criteria #2: Assessments are open-ended whenever possible. The activities give each student the opportunity to show all that he or she knows and is capable of doing.

Criteria #3: Assessments incorporate a range of standards in any given content area. Consider what students can do in the content area and, if applicable, integrate those standards into other content areas.

Criteria #4: Assessments are relevant and appropriate. The purpose of each activity is clear to students, and the activities are developmentally appropriate.

Criteria #5: Assessments reflect the many ways in which children learn. Choose activities that allow the uses of varied learning styles and multiple intelligences. As stated in "Learning to Love Assessment" (Tomlinson 2007), "when one form of assessment was ineffective for a student, it did not necessarily indicate a lack of student success but could, in fact, represent a poor fit between the student and the method through which I was trying to make the student communicate."

These criteria should be followed as a rule. But formative assessments can be formal (e.g., those created by teacher teams and distributed among teachers for the purpose of standardization and consistency). These assessments are contrived. Make these the exception, though, not the rule. Why? In a differentiated classroom environment where students are showing what they know in different ways and are given more than one opportunity to show new levels of understanding, formal assessments may not always be appropriate. In this case, formal assessments become the minority tools. Authentic assessments become the majority.

Student-Created Products and Menus

Assessments come in many forms. Student-created products can be used as pre-, formative, and summative assessments. Although most teachers I work with are open to the idea, I have been in conversation with many who have said, "The students are making posters, diagrams, pictures, poems, raps, and journals as assessments? That sounds like fluff. We are wasting precious time with that because when our students get into the real world, they *won't* be doing those things."

Don't bet on that. I can tell you what they *won't* be doing in the real world when they leave school and get jobs. They won't be taking tests to show their bosses what they know. They will be creating products. Building cars. Fixing engines. Designing bridges. Writing business reports. Cooking four-course meals. Performing songs. Painting pictures. Making and flipping hamburgers. The only time they will be taking tests is when they are applying to get into programs, such as college or technical school or to get a driver's license (and even then they are required to also drive the car). Your students will be creating products for the rest of their lives. Allow them to show what they know based on this idea of modeling what they will be doing in the real world and giving them choices based on their strengths. Indeed, research reveals that we tend to pick our careers based on these strengths (Armstrong 1994). As you begin to implement these authentic forms of assessment, you may find that the data is much richer than what you would receive from a less flexible method of assessment. An *Educational Leadership* article written by Robert Marzano (1994) investigates the use of authentic assessments among a group of teachers and found that more than two-thirds of them said that the authentic tasks provided them with better assessment data than when they used more traditional forms of assessment.

On the subject of tests, I understand the reality that in school systems, all students take standardized tests at one time or another. I don't want to exclude paper-pencil, fill-in-the-bubble, or fill-in-the-blank forms of assessment from your list. Assessments come in many forms, and they include these types of tests and quizzes. No matter how much you may agree or disagree with the validity of these types of tests, the reality is that they are real and students have to take them. It is often mandated. So do students a favor by including assessments like these every now and then in the formative and summative stages. These assessments do still give you the data you need to drive instruction, and they will also give students the chance to practice these forms of assessment in preparation for standardized, high-stakes tests.

Let's look again at the possible products that students can create for formative assessment. Figure 3.1 lists products that can be used as assessments.

Figure 3.1 Student-Created Products as Assessments

advertisement	game	picture story for children
alphabet board	graph	play
animated movie	hidden picture	poetry
annotated bibliography	illustrated story	pop-up book
art gallery	interview	PowerPoint® slideshow
bulletin board	journal	press conference
chart	labeled diagram	puppet
choral reading	large-scale drawing	puppet show
clay sculpture	lesson	puzzle
collage	letter	radio program
comic strip	map with legend	report
costume	mazes	riddle
crossword puzzle	model	role-play
debate	mural	sculpture
demonstration	museum exhibit	skit
detailed illustration	music	slideshow
diary	needlework	slogan
editorial essay	newspaper story	song
experiment	oral report	survey
fairy tale	painting	television program
family tree	pamphlet	time line
film	papier-mâché	travel brochure
filmstrip	petition	voice recording
flip book	photo essay	write a new law

Student Product Menus

Student product menus can be created from the list of products shown in Figure 3.1. Menus in restaurants allow customers to view their choices and select from those choices. The same goes for student product menus. Students view the list and choose how they want to show what they know about content. Since the point of assessment is to see what a student knows about content, then how the student shows this can be offered up as a choice. Of course, there will be times when the teacher wants to make that choice for the student, but no matter which product is chosen, content understanding is what the teacher will evaluate in the end.

Asking students to mark their choices on a menu before beginning the assessment may alleviate the stress that comes from asking a student to show understanding in a mode that is difficult for him or her (e.g., the struggling writer who can more accurately depict answers through pictures or diagrams). Also, marking choices on a menu before beginning the assessment helps to save time. Students often waste time staring blankly as they

Figure 3.2 Student Product Menu 1

Appendix A • Additional Resources

Student Product Menu 1

Name: ______________________

Content/Standard: ______________________

Directions: Check the box that tells how you will show the information you know.

- ❑ Draw a picture.
- ❑ Act it out.
- ❑ Write a letter.
- ❑ Write a song and sing it.
- ❑ Tell the teacher.

My idea: ______________________

• 165

Figure 3.3 Student Product Menu 2

Appendix A • Additional Resources

Student Product Menu 2

Name: ______________________

Content/Standard: ______________________

Directions: Check the box that tells you how you will show the information you know.

❑ comic strip	❑ pamphlet
❑ detailed illustration	❑ poetry
❑ diary entry	❑ short essay
❑ flip book	❑ song
❑ graph	❑ radio program
❑ illustrated story	❑ time line
❑ letter	❑ voice recording
❑ painting	❑ other

My idea: ______________________

166 •

try to decide what to do. With a product menu checklist in front of them, they see their options and mark their choices quickly. For students who still have a hard time choosing, even from a menu, you can highlight three or four options from which to choose.

Try to keep the product menus that you create for your class as generic as possible. This will prevent you from having to create a new product menu for every assignment. For example, instead of *editorial essay*, say *essay* or *written document*.

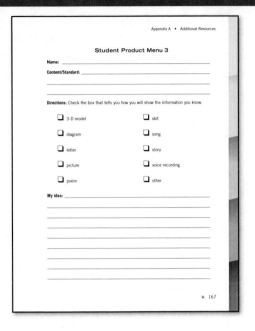

Figure 3.4 Student Product Menu 3

Figures 3.2, 3.3, and 3.4—*Student Product Menu 1*, *Student Product Menu 2*, and *Student Product Menu 3*, respectively—are examples of generic student product menus. *Student Product Menu 1* is for younger students; *Student Product Menu 2* and *Student Product Menu 3* are for older students. You can look at the menus and decide which is the most developmentally appropriate for your students. These templates can be found in Appendix A.

Differentiated Assessments

Differentiated assessments are often activities that have both teacher choice and student choice built into the structure. With this type of assessment, the teacher determines the thinking skill and the content based on the standards, which are the same for all students. Students choose the method of research and the product. These student choices allow for differentiation as opposed to traditional assessments where students all do the same thing at the same time in the same way.

Differentiated assessments can be either formative or summative. I will talk about them as formative or assigned during the practice phase of the learning curve. Of course, they would be summative if given when students are at the top of the learning curve in their understanding of the concept.

The following are examples of differentiated assessments. These are teacher's plans; students will see only the thinking skill and content in the form of directions for the assessment. Following the examples is a breakdown of each component (i.e., Thinking Skill, Content, Research Skills, and Product).

Differentiated Assessment Example #1

1. Process: Thinking Skill (Bloom's Taxonomy)	2. Content: Standards-based	3. Process: Research Skills (Research Sources)	4. Product: Evidence of Understanding
determine	the characteristics of mammals	students choose from a research checklist	students choose from a product checklist

Differentiated Assessment Example #2

1. Process: Thinking Skill (Bloom's Taxonomy)	2. Content: Standards-based	3. Process: Research Skills (Research Sources)	4. Product: Evidence of Understanding
describe	the causes and effects of the Industrial Revolution	students choose from a research checklist	students choose from a product checklist

Differentiated Assessment Example #3

1. Process: Thinking Skill (Bloom's Taxonomy)	2. Content: Standards-based	3. Process: Research Skills (Research Sources)	4. Product: Evidence of Understanding
examine	how each main character (choose at least two) contributed to the conflict in the story	students choose from a research checklist	students choose from a product checklist

1. **Process: Thinking Skill**—The verbs used here come from the categories of thinking described in Bloom's Taxonomy (Bloom and Krathwohl 1984). There are six categories: remembering, understanding, applying, analyzing, evaluating, and creating. Figure 3.5 lists verbs you can use for the *Thinking Skill* box in the examples above. The verbs in the chart are based on the work of Anderson and Krathwohl (2000).

Figure 3.5 Verbs to Use at Each Level of Bloom's Taxonomy

Remembering—Can the student recall or remember the information?

check	list	name	repeat
choose	locate	read	reproduce
find	match	recall	show
label	memorize	recite	state

Understanding—Can the student explain ideas or concepts?

account for	define	qualify	show
alter	interpret	recognize	translate
change	paraphrase	retell	

Applying—Can the student use the information in a new way?

adopt	employ	relate	solve
diagram	illustrate	report	use

Analyzing—Can the student distinguish among the different parts?

categorize	contrast	dissect	inspect
classify	differentiate	distinguish	simplify
compare	discriminate	examine	uncover

Evaluating—Can the student justify a stand or decision?

appraise	determine	rank	select
criticize	grade	recommend	support
debate	judge	reject	

Creating—Can the student create a new product or point of view?

combine	create	formulate	produce
compose	design	invent	reorder
construct	develop	predict	reorganize

2. **Content**—Content here is the standard(s) being measured in this assessment.

3. **Process: Research Skills**—How will each student gather the information about the content? Research choices can be available in a research menu (see Figure 3.6). Research choices may be posted in the classroom. Keep in mind that you have the option to limit the number of choices on this menu or even choose which mode of research you want students to use. This resource can be found in Appendix A.

Figure 3.6 Research Menu

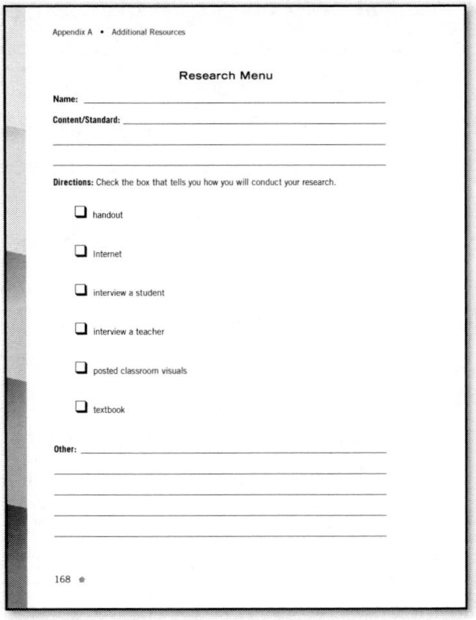

Appendix A • Additional Resources

Research Menu

Name: ______

Content/Standard: ______

Directions: Check the box that tells you how you will conduct your research.

- ❑ handout
- ❑ Internet
- ❑ interview a student
- ❑ interview a teacher
- ❑ posted classroom visuals
- ❑ textbook

Other: ______

168

4. **Product**—How will students show their understanding of the content? Student product menus should be available to students as they select their product for the assessment. Again, you have the option to limit the number of choices on this menu. You also have the option to choose the product for students, but if you do so, remember to keep students' learning modalities in mind. These are differentiated assessments, so it is best to let students choose whenever possible.

Tiered Assessments

Tiered assessments are almost always formative. They are created as a result of data gathered from recent formative assessments.

A teacher should tier an assessment when he or she sees that after reviewing the data, there are significant gaps in students' understanding of a concept that has just been taught. In evaluating these gaps in understanding, the teacher realizes that some students need more time on the basic understanding of the concept while others understand and are ready for higher levels of application. Tiered assessments allow for all students to practice the same content but at varying levels of depth and complexity.

Let's see how this looks in the classroom. After a whole-group lesson followed by formative assessment, you find that there are ten students who are still struggling with the content, twelve who seem to have a pretty good understanding and are ready to apply the content, and two who clearly have a firm grasp on the content and are ready for much more complex application. In this case, your plan would be to tier the next assessment into three levels of depth and complexity to meet the needs of all three groups of students.

What Do Tiered Assessments Look Like?

The first level of a tiered assessment looks like the basic differentiated assignment sample described previously. The next levels take that basic concept into varying levels of depth and complexity.

Key elements of tiered assessments:

- Grade-level standards, concepts, and/or essential skills are identified and targeted

- Content is modified into two or three progressive levels of depth and complexity

- Students' learning modalities are accommodated by offering choices for research and product

The resulting student-created products from all levels of the tiered assessment are the data that will indicate students' understanding of the content.

Samples of a teacher's plans for tiered assessments are found here and on the following page. Students will see only the thinking skill and content in the form of directions for the assignment for their level only. And as with differentiated assessments, student product checklists should be available to students as they select their product for the tiered assessment.

As you look at the samples, note that it is not the *content* that is modified into levels of depth and complexity but the *thinking skill*. Also note that the content language (which is bold in these examples) remains the same throughout each tier because students' understanding of this content is what will be measured. For example, in the first sample, you are measuring student's knowledge of mammal characteristics only, not how the characteristics compare to one another or how the habitats correlate. Those tasks require the student to apply the content. For every tier, measure students only on the targeted standards-based content.

Example Tiered Assessment Teacher Plan: Mammal Characteristics

1. Process: Thinking Skill (Bloom's Taxonomy)	2. Content (Standards-based)	3. Process: Research Skills (Research Sources)	4. Product (Evidence of Understanding)
determine	the **characteristics of mammals**	students choose from research checklist	students choose from product checklist
compare/contrast	the **characteristics of mammals** with those of another class of animal	students choose from research checklist	students choose from product checklist
examine	how each of the **characteristics of mammals** correlates with their environments	students choose from research checklist	students choose from product checklist

Example Tiered Assessment Teacher Plan: Industrial Revolution

1. Process: Thinking Skill (Bloom's Taxonomy)	2. Content (Standards-based)	3. Process: Research Skills (Research Sources)	4. Product (Evidence of Understanding)
describe	the **causes and effects of the Industrial Revolution**	students choose from research checklist	students choose from product checklist
categorize	the **causes and effects of the Industrial Revolution** by their positive or negative impact on society	students choose from research checklist	students choose from product checklist
judge with evidence	how patterns in the behaviors of consumers and producers contributed to the **causes and effects of the Industrial Revolution**	students choose from research checklist	students choose from product checklist

Homework as Assessment

A Traditional Perspective

Sometimes I beat myself up (rhetorically speaking, of course) when I think about what I used to do in my early years of teaching—especially when it came to homework! I realize, however, that as teachers, we do what we think is best for students with the information we have at the time. This is why it is important for teachers to not only keep up with current research and pedagogies but also to use good judgment and common sense!

I remember during the first week of a new school year, I would show students what an extremely low grade on homework would do to otherwise high grades when they were averaged together. I wrote a list of grades on the board and asked them to find the average, making sure that the average would result in a high grade. Then, I stuck a big, fat zero in the list and asked them to average the grades again. With shock and horror, students saw that adding the zero brought the average grade down considerably. For example, by adding that zero, a high score of 85 percent plummeted to a 60 percent! Then I would snarl (I always used theatrics to drive a point), "See what happens to a good grade when you don't turn in your homework?" Little did I realize I was creating a classroom of frightened students who as a result of my fear tactics would be forever fixated on scores rather than content.

A Common Sense Perspective

I know better now. As I chalked up more experience in the classroom and learned more about formative and summative assessment, I applied common sense to the issue of homework. Homework is practice. Homework informs the teacher about how students are doing on understanding a concept. Homework informs the teacher on how to plan future instruction and what students need. Homework is formative and therefore should not be included in the mix when averaging grades for final reporting purposes.

As I mentioned in Chapter 2, I understand that sometimes you do not have choices in this matter because of grade book or reporting restrictions. However, this approach to homework is consistent with the common sense perspective of this book. Do what you can to maintain common sense as you adhere to these restrictions when making decisions about homework.

What Does Homework Look Like?

Homework is practice (e.g., writing, drawing, diagrams, models) that did not get completed in class. Or it is practice that is purposefully assigned by the teacher for students to do at home. I have used it both ways, but personally I prefer the latter. Homework for my students was practice that could only be done at home. For example, when our unit of study was astronomy and the standard was identifying stars and constellations, the students built sextons in class. Their task at home was to locate the North Star using their sextons, diagram what they saw, and write their explanations in their science journals. The diagrams and journal entries were the products I used to assess and evaluate their understanding of the standard. Another example was when I asked my students to interview their parents on a topic related to a current unit of study. This type of practice can *only* be done at home. It would definitely be *home*work. Purposefully assigning homework is essential to the common sense perspective, and this idea will be developed further in this section.

Grading Homework

When given a homework assignment, students typically ask, "Are we going to get a grade for this?" Why do they ask this question? Usually, it's because they want to know how much effort to put into their work. If it gets a grade, they put forth effort. If it doesn't get a grade, they translate that the task is not important and therefore do not put forth effort.

Teachers have well intendedly but inadvertently created *Whadja get?* monsters, and it only gets worse as the years roll on. By middle and high school, students have learned to manipulate the system by working the numbers. Without realizing it, teachers have actually taught students to do this by negotiating and offering deals, such as, "If you get 85 percent or above on your quizzes, you can skip the final," or, "Your homework grades count for 40 percent of your final grade." And so on. We've created grade-manipulating monsters (figuratively speaking, of course) who don't have a clue why they are doing the work. They just know that they have to do it in order to make the grade. It's been drilled into their brains.

Of course, these are general statements. There are always students who genuinely love to learn, and it is the joy of the challenge that keeps these students going. These are the students who ask for homework when none is assigned or ask for even more when it is assigned.

So how do I respond when my students ask if they will receive a grade for their homework? I say, "Yes." And it's the truth. Every assessment should be evaluated, and formative assessments are no exception. That evaluation may come in the form of a grade, a check mark, a smiley face, etc. So I am sincere when I tell them they will, indeed, get a grade or some form of evaluation. I also make sure to tell them that they are held accountable for every assignment.

Keeping Track

Homework is a type of formative assessment. Therefore, it is important to keep track of homework completion and scores to monitor student learning. Checklists are great accountability tools for this purpose. Create a checklist for every formative assignment or activity that students are accountable for in a given grading period. Put a check mark or even a grade in the box next to each assignment on the list. Using a fractional form (e.g., 4 out of 5 correct) says much more for remediation purposes than a letter grade. And that's what formative assessments are for; they are the red flags for driving future instruction. Homework is no exception. Homework assignments are checkpoints along the journey to the top of the learning curve. When there is an absence of a check mark on that list of formative assignments, which includes homework, there needs to be a consequence that is determined by you. Just remember that the threat of a lower grade on the report card should not be one of them.

So where do you record formative assessments (including homework)? You can record them in a grade book as you may have always done. The only difference now is that the scores for formative assessments, including homework, are kept separate from summative grades. By doing so, you can look for patterns as students practice their skills that are tied to the content standards. Here is where you can see formative evaluation patterns that will indicate how you can group students for remediation in specific areas of need (more about this later in this chapter). Keeping track of formative assessments in isolation is an effective way to use the data to plan for future instruction.

Providing Immediate Feedback

All formative assessments, including homework, should be evaluated quickly, and immediate feedback should be given to students. Formative assessments not only inform your instruction, but they also inform students as to whether they need to practice further or move on.

Consensus checking is one effective strategy for providing immediate feedback on classroom assignments or homework. It also provides an opportunity for students to interact with the content through collaboration and discussion. This strategy takes some time, but when you think about how long it takes you to grade work, return it to students, and then confer with them on their progress, the time invested here is well spent. Here, students check and evaluate their assignments by consensus. This is how it works:

1. In groups of three or four, students compare their work with the other members of the group, one problem/item at a time.

2. Students discuss any discrepancies, working through each problem until everyone is in agreement. (*Note:* Talk to students beforehand about the possibility that one person may have the accurate answer and the rest may not.)

3. Individuals make necessary revisions to their work as the process continues. Students use highlighters to indicate which problems were revised. This helps the teacher and students see where more practice may be needed.

4. If at any time students are at an impasse, the student who is not in agreement will make note of the disagreement on his or her work.

5. Students continue this process until all items have been checked. Students endorse each member's paper by signing their initials. This endorsement symbolizes an agreement that the signer would claim that paper as his or her own. Students do not have to endorse papers that they disagreed with and/or where revisions were not made.

6. The teacher collects the papers for evaluation and further feedback and uses the data for future instruction.

The benefits of checking by consensus are huge. Some of these benefits are highlighted:

- "We learn 70% of what we discuss with others" (Glasser 1969). This is done with consensus checking.

- "We learn 95% of what we teach to someone else" (Glasser 1969). This is done with consensus checking.

- Instant feedback. This is done with consensus checking.

- Students benefit from a pinch of peer pressure to have classroom assignments and homework completed for this activity.

Consensus Checking—Potential Problems to Be Addressed:

- **What if students do not mark the answers they've revised in order to have more correct answers than they actually had?** The potential for this is small when the papers are checked in groups of three or four students. Everyone is watching! By this time, you will have made clear that these are formative and the grades serve as guides for you to direct your instruction.

- **What if students arrive at the wrong consensus? Wouldn't they then continue to believe the wrong information?** The purpose of formative assessment is to drive future instruction and to provide feedback for students regarding their understanding of the content. Therefore, you will collect the work after the consensus activity, evaluate each student's product, and then adjust subsequent instruction *immediately* to correct any misconceptions. These corrections are also noted on the assessment itself. Consensus checking does not let the teacher off the evaluation hook!

Student Writing

Writing across the content areas is a powerful tool for determining content understanding. The following are key points to consider when using writing for formative assessment:

When to Use Writing for Assessment

- Use writing when a student wants to write a personal note to the teacher, such as "This was hard," "I get it now!" "I need help," or "This was too easy for me." These notes can be written on sticky notes and attached to the product or written on the product itself. You should respond to at least some or all of the notes to show students that you are actually reading them. These notes are effective forms of formative assessment as they get students to think about what they understand about the assignment while they are completing it and reflect on what they learned when they are finished.

- Use writing when students are asked to explain strategies or processes that were used to complete a task or solve a problem across the content areas. Asking students to explain or justify their thinking is a great tool to help you understand their depth of knowledge around a concept or standard.

- Use writing when students are asked to reflect on a lesson in a journal. This uses the "notes to the teacher" strategy described in the first bullet to a more in-depth level in the form of journal writing. Students have more room to write personal feelings and reflections in a journal. Journals are safe havens for reflection as the promise is that only the teacher will read it.

Why Use Writing for Assessment?

- Writing can be used to assess student understanding of essential concepts.

- Writing responses to questions or explaining strategies gives students opportunities to improve communication skills and think clearly about what they are learning.

- Writing helps students clarify their responses to problems.

- Writing helps students discover mistakes in reasoning when a written response is followed by verbally sharing this response with an individual or a group. Verbalizing written responses to others also puts the student into a teaching position. This supports William Glasser's learning theory, which states that "we learn 95% of what we teach to the others" (1969).

What to Look for in Written Responses

- *What* is the solution or answer? This is where the student gives his or her "final answer."

- *How* did the student arrive at the solution or answer? Here the student describes the process he or she used to find the solution to the problem or answer to the question.

- *Why* did the student use this process? Wherever the student tells *how*, there must be a reason *why* that choice was made. As suggested in the preceding section, answering these questions helps students clarify their responses to problems.

The following example shows how writing helped the teacher to assess a student's understanding of the content. The content area is mathematics, and the targeted standard involves perimeter. Students were presented with the problem scenario and asked to solve it. The questions at the end of the example were used to help the teacher analyze student responses. Those questions can be transferred to use in your classroom as you evaluate students' explanations.

The problem: Your class is collecting canned foods for a community project. Your teacher has found space to store the cans in an unused area of the playground. The space designated in this area is 12 feet long and 9 feet wide. Your class decides to block off this space by putting a small wire fence around it. How much fencing will be needed?

Kayla's response: 43 feet

Her teacher, Mr. Marsh, was ready to mark this as incorrect. He decided to ask Kayla to write an explanation for her answer, making sure to include *how* and *why*. She wrote, "I added 18 feet and 24 feet because that is the total measurement of all four sides. (This answers *how* and *why*.) The answer is 42 feet. (This is the solution.) I added one more foot because I wanted to make sure there would be enough fencing. So I got 43."

Questions to consider for guiding learning and instruction:

1. What would your evaluation be of Kayla's understanding of perimeter? *(Possible answer: She does understand because she explained the process she used to find the perimeter of the storage space, which was correct.)*

2. How could Kayla have deepened the description of her process? *(Possible answer: Her description included the* what, how, *and* why, *so the description was clear and deep. She even explained the extra foot at the end. All bases were covered!)*

3. How would you direct your instruction for Kayla at this point? *(Possible answer: Instruct her to read the problem carefully and stay with what is asked rather than adding on extra fencing.)*

What the teacher accomplished with this process is a fine example of using data to guide learning and instruction. He evaluated the data, guided the student's learning by asking for clarification through writing, and prepared himself for future instruction for Kayla based on areas where she needed to improve.

Journal Writing

Journal writing makes a great bell-ringer activity. Bell-ringer activities are designed to engage students during transitions between lessons or right after the bell rings for class to begin. It can also be effective as an activity to close the last few minutes of class as it gives students the chance to reflect on what was learned and provides the teacher with insight about what students need academically and even emotionally. Journal writing can expose the deepest feelings of inadequacy or trepidation students may be harboring. The teacher can detect if students are bored or frustrated. Journals are safe venues for reflection. They are chances to "talk" to the teacher without confrontation. Journals are formative assessments and should be taken seriously as a form of data to use to plan future instruction.

When using journals as formative assessments, be specific about what you want students to write. Journal starters should focus on content standards for assessment purposes, but realize that general journal starters about feelings and emotions are also appropriate as well.

Figures 3.7 and 3.8 are some sample journal starters that reflect on understanding content as well as the student's feelings and even the classroom learning environment.

Figure 3.7 Journal Starters for Concept Understanding

What I like best about this activity is...

What I like least about this activity is...

My favorite part of this lesson is _____ because...

If I could redo this activity, some new materials I would use would be...

The most important thing I learned (today, this week, this month) is...

The part of this activity that I feel most comfortable with is...

If I could be any story character, I would be _____ because...

One thing I achieved in math (science, reading, etc.) this week is...

If I could change one thing about this activity, it would be...

When I work with a group, I feel...

When I show my ideas to the class, I feel...

During this past week, I used science (math, literacy skills, history, etc.) outside the classroom to...

I make the most errors on _____ because...

Another example of today's lesson in _____ is...

If I could work further on this problem/project, I would...

What is easy in this activity is...

What I still don't understand or need more practice in is...

Figure 3.8 Content-Area Journal Starters

I would like to work with _____ as a partner because...

What things did you like about working in a _____ group? Dislike?

What did you do in _____ class today?

Today I learned...

The most important thing to remember about today's _____ lesson is...

How and when might you use the _____ that you learned today?

Make up three questions for your next _____ test.

My goal for this week in _____ is...

What are your _____ goals for the year?

Describe how _____ is similar to other school subjects. How is it different?

What's the most difficult thing for you to do in _____?

What can you do to make fewer mistakes in _____?

When I have _____ homework, I...

What is the one thing about _____ that you like best?

Choose a sample of your best work. What is it? Why did you select it as your best work?

What is the one thing about _____ that you like least?

Write a letter to your teacher comparing your progress in _____ this year to your progress last year.

Explain in a note to an absent classmate what was done in _____ class today.

More Formative Assessment Strategies

The following are additional assessment strategies you can use for formative assessment of students' understanding of content. In each case, students' responses are the formative assessments. The resulting data serves to show where students are in understanding the content/targeted standards. Use this data to plan future instruction.

Strategy: Responding to Text

Grade Levels

K–12

Materials

- appropriate piece of text
- *Activity Response Sheet 1* or *Activity Response Sheet 2* (Appendix A)

Procedure

Note: We can assess students' understanding of content when they provide us with specific evidence of their thinking by responding to text. They can show us their knowledge by answering questions during reading conferences to illustrate their thinking. This can be used with fiction, nonfiction, and/or content-area texts.

1. Read a piece of text with students.

2. Ask students questions about the text.

3. Have students respond to the questions verbally, on their activity response sheets, or by placing a sticky note next to the text that illustrates their thoughts.

Activity Response Sheet 1 **Activity Response Sheet 2**

The following are examples of questions to ask students so that they respond to the text appropriately.

Making connections: Is there a part of this story that reminds you of something in your life or of something that has happened to you?

Questioning: Can you show me a part of the text where you have a question? What were you wondering as you read this part? Is there a part where you were confused? What was confusing about it?

Visualizing: Were there places in the story where you made a picture in your mind? What images did you see?

Inferring: What do you predict will happen in this story? Can you show me in the text where you found yourself making an inference?

Determining importance: What is this story about? What are some of the most important or interesting ideas that struck you? What do you think is the most important thing to remember about this story?

Synthesizing: Can you tell me what the story is about in just a few sentences? Can you show me a place in the text where you changed your mind? What changed your mind? Do you have some new ideas or information?

Have students answer these questions using sticky notes, charts, or response sheets. Response sheets are handouts, formatted with lines or boxes on which students can respond to a hands-on, center-type activity with written or illustrated responses. (See *Activity Response Sheet 1* and *Activity Response Sheet 2* in Appendix A.) This encourages students to use evidence and examples that build meaning and limit irrelevant responses.

Strategy: Chocolate Pudding Vocabulary

Grade Levels	Materials
K–12	• chocolate pudding (approximately 1 cup per student)
	• antibacterial hand sanitizer

Procedure

Note: In preparation, cover each student's desk with wax paper.

1. Ladle chocolate pudding onto each student's desk.

2. Have students wipe their hands with antibacterial hand sanitizer. Explain the rule that no one touches another person's pudding.

3. Instruct students to write a content vocabulary word in the chocolate pudding with one finger. As an option, when time and space allow for it, students can write in their pudding with their noses! This appeals to the naturalist/environmental intelligence in which stimulating the senses helps the brain learn.

4. With partners, or on a separate response sheet, have students explain the meaning of the vocabulary word and how they have used the word in context during the course of the week.

5. Have students "erase" the words by gently wiping their hand across the pudding to smooth it out.

6. Repeat this process with additional vocabulary words.

Strategy: Tac-Toes

Grade Levels

K–12

Materials

_____ *Tac-Toe* (Appendix A)

Procedure

Note: Any content-area activities can be put into the Tac-Toe format. The activities can be depicted in words or, for nonreaders, pictures.

1. Create a Tac-Toe board using the _____ *Tac-Toe* template.

_____-Tac-Toe

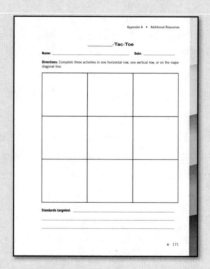

2. Distribute a copy of the board to each student.

3. Have students choose and complete all assessment activities on the horizontal row, the vertical column, or along the major diagonal.

4. When students have completed one line, they may choose another line, if directed to do so by the teacher.

Tac-Toes can be used in any content area. The activities are short and simple but not necessarily easy. The activities should not take the student too long to complete. These are practice activities, not projects. Focus on the standards in the activities you choose. Having trouble finding assessment activities to put inside the boxes? Look into the repertoire of classroom activities that you have already been using. Network with other teachers and gather more ideas for more activities. Go online and look for Tac-Toe ideas. Be sure when you go to your search engine that you type in a specific content area like *Math–Tac–Toe* or *Reading–Tac–Toe*.

Figures 3.9 and 3.10 are examples of Tac-Toe boards. General topics have been listed; however, when you create a Tac-Toe, you may want to list the actual standard below the chart. These resources can be found in Appendix A in addition to a blank _____ *Tac-Toe* template.

Figure 3.9 Math-Tac-Toe

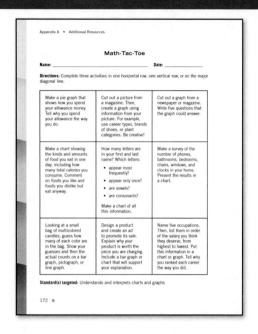

Figure 3.10 Reading-Tac-Toe

Strategy: Student-Created *I Have, Who Has* Cards

Grade Levels	Materials
K–12	*I Have, Who Has?* cards

Procedure

Note: This strategy is a great ongoing assessment activity that engages all learners and provides students with guided practice time. Cards are made up with statements and questions that pertain to a current standards-based unit of study. The total number of cards is determined by the student and/or teacher.

1. The student writes on each card an *I Have, Who Has?* statement and question. For example, if the standard is U.S. states and capitals, the question would be, "Who has the capital of Arizona?" The corresponding statement—written on the top of a new card—would be, "I have Phoenix." See Figure 3.11 for how the statements are set up. The completed cards are collected and their contents evaluated by the teacher before being used as a learning game. The questions and answers written on the cards are the formative assessment.

2. To use the cards as a learning game, give each student one card. One student starts by separating himself or herself from the other students and reading his or her question aloud on the card. (e.g., "Who has [reads the question on the card]?")

3. The student with the *Who Has?* question answers by reading: "I have [reads the answer on the card]." This student then joins the first student. The students place themselves so as to form a circle. This process continues until the answer to the final question is answered by the first. The circle is now complete!

Figure 3.11 shows a sample set of cards created from the book *Charlotte's Web* by E. B. White. Just a few of the cards are shown, so you can see the pattern of how they are created.

Figure 3.11 Sample *I Have, Who Has?* Cards

I have "some pig." Who has the rat?	I have Wilbur will be butchered. Who has the solution to Wilbur's problem?
I have Templeton. Who has Wilbur's problem?	I have Wilbur will be made to be important. Who has Charlotte's first words for the web?

Evaluating Formative Assessments

If I've heard it once, I've heard it a thousand times from teachers all over the country. I even remember these words coming out of my own mouth many years ago. "I'd love to differentiate instruction, but I don't know how to grade students when everyone is doing something different! It's much easier to grade when students are doing the same thing at the same time in the same way."

With those words, then, teachers go back to traditional, whole-group instruction where products are the same and the grading is thus standardized. I can't blame them; it does seem overwhelming when you have twenty-five or more students in your class and you may be teaching five or more classes. Human nature tends to steer us down the path of least resistance (Fritz 1989). If this is true, then after all the training on authentic assessment and differentiated instruction, the tendency for overwhelmed teachers is to revert back to what seems easiest (i.e., standardized assessments, which beget standardized grading).

Measure Students Against the Standard

There is one simple statement that might help get things into a common-sense perspective and still steer you down a peaceful path. On any assessment, measure students against the standard, not each other.

So, whether students choose to make a poster, draw a diagram, write a letter, or conduct a mammal-on-the-street interview, you are looking for understanding of content. The content is the standard. The standard is the *same* for everyone. In the poster, did the student show the five characteristics of a mammal? Did the student who created the diagram also show those five characteristics? How about the mammal-on-the-street interview? Were all five characteristics mentioned? The content is always standard, and that forms the basis for the evaluation.

Consider this example: If the content says there are five characteristics, then each characteristic can be assigned 20 points to equal a total of 100. You can turn those points into a percentage if you wish. No matter what the product, the accuracy of the content will be measured by 20s up to 100 for every student.

Accuracy of Content Versus Quality of Product

Now, what about the student (I'll call him Raj) who spends a lot of time perfecting his poster on the five characteristics? Raj takes pains to color within the lines, and he uses his very best handwriting, labeling each characteristic with utmost care. The teacher scores his product, seeing that he identified four out of five mammal characteristics. Since the teacher is measuring the student against the standard, Raj receives an 80 percent on content.

Then there's another student in the same class (I'll call him Lyle). Lyle decides to write a letter as one mammal to another. He slaps a few lines on a sheet of paper with a dull pencil. His words are hard to read since he decided to scratch out words rather than erase them. His dog played tug-of-war with this assignment, and Lyle finally won the war just in time to turn in the wrinkled mess to the teacher. The teacher scores his product, seeing that he identified four out of five mammal characteristics. Since she is measuring the student against the standard, Lyle, too, receives an 80 percent on content.

But is this fair? Judging students on mastery of the content is indeed fair. Is it right? Considering that they both correctly identified four of the five mammal characteristics, yes, it is right because the score accurately reflects students' understanding of the content. But is there more to this? Yes! There is a saying regarding human nature that goes like this: "People behave the way you treat them." The behavior in your classroom is no exception. If you accept "junk," you will most likely get "junk." The adverse is true as well. If you expect quality, you will get quality. Students will produce for you whatever you have set as a standard for them. I'm not talking about standards for *content* here; I'm talking about standards for *quality*. Your students will rise to meet the bar that you set for them. If you set it low, they will aim low. If you set it high, they will aim high.

To set the bar, create specific criteria for quality work. Let students help decide what should be on that list. Create a poster that bullets criteria for quality work. Make the list generic so that the criteria can apply to just about any assessment type, remembering that assessments come in many forms.

Figure 3.12 shows an example of a quality criteria sheet, followed by a list of other possible criteria. I highly suggest that you let the students help decide what the quality criteria should be. The more involved they are in creating this list, the more buy-in they have and thus the more likely they will be to take this process seriously when they create their products. Make sure that the criteria are generic so that a new list does not have to be recreated with every assessment. Modify the language to suit your grade level, and change the format to suit your needs as well. Remember, people behave the way you treat them. So don't accept products that do not have all boxes checked! This resource can be found in Appendix A.

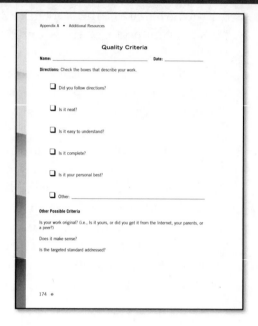

Figure 3.12 Quality Criteria

Model the Criteria

Students need to see and understand what each criterion is asking for. Role-play your expectations. Show examples. Do not assume that students know what you mean when you say *neat*, *complete*, or *personal best*. The following descriptions will help you with your models:

Did you follow directions?

This refers to everything you've asked them to do on the assignment as far as process goes. Did they put their names on their papers? Did they compare and forget to contrast? Is the written assignment the required length?

Is it neat?

This criterion covers a lot of ground. It considers differences among students. What is considered neat for one student might not necessarily be the same for another. Every student's level of neatness will vary. You know what a student is capable of in this area. That student also knows what he or she is capable of. As the year rolls on, students' classmates know what each of their peers is capable of as well.

Is it easy to understand?

This addresses how well the message comes across in the product. Is the poster so full of information that it reminds you of a Where's Waldo® puzzle? Is the voice on the recording muffled? Is the student speaking so rapidly that his or her words are hard to decipher?

Is it complete?

This criterion speaks for itself. Did the student finish the assignment? Are all parts present and accounted for?

Is it your personal best?

This final criterion addresses a general look at the choices a student has made. Does the chosen product or aspects of the product match the student's developmental capabilities? For example, if the directions for finding the main character in a story say to "choose a book," did the student choose a story at his or her reading level? If Marlene, who reads at a sixth grade level, chooses a second grade book, she is not doing her personal best. Or if Alex, who writes prose at a high school level, chooses to scribble down a few phrases on a sheet of paper when asked to describe the causes and effects of the Civil War, he is not doing his personal best.

Keep Content Scores and Quality Scores Separate

The evaluation of content is scored separately from the evaluation for quality. There will be two evaluations for the assessment, one for quality of the product and one for the accuracy of the content. If there are five criteria listed, each is worth 20 points or 20 percent for a total of 100 percent.

So very often I have seen teachers lower students' scores because they didn't put their name on their papers. In fact, I beat myself up for having done this myself years ago before I adopted the common-sense approach! Yes, following directions is important, as are all the other quality criteria. By evaluating the two separately, however, you are making it clear to students that not only is quality important but so is accuracy of the content.

Let's take Lyle's product, the letter. He received an 80 percent on content. His product wasn't easy to understand, and it certainly wasn't neat or his personal best, so he ended up with a 40 percent on quality. If those two scores are averaged, which is traditionally done in order to end up with one score, Lyle ends up with a nebulous 60 percent on the assessment as a whole. By averaging the two scores, what have we just done with those two valuable pieces of information (i.e., that he knows the content and the quality)? We have muddied the data waters! We've combined apples and oranges and made murky fruit juice. Now the parents, student, or anyone else who looks at the score doesn't know if Lyle needs help with content or if he needs help with product quality. If you keep the evaluations separate, you will know how to drive future instruction with the Lyles, the Rajs, and everyone else in your classroom.

Figure 3.13 Standards-Based Scoring of Formative/Summative Assessments Sample

Figure 3.13 shows a standards-based evaluation format for both formative and summative assessments. For formative assessments, the data is used to drive future instruction and learning. For summative assessments, the data is used on a final reporting document. Check marks, fractions, or symbols may be used in place of points or percentages. A blank template of this form is found in Appendix A.

Standards-Based Scoring of Formative/Summative Assessments

Name: Lyle Smith   Date: 10/12/2012

Content/Standards: Mammal Characteristics

Key Content (Based on the Standard)	Evaluation
1. Warm Blooded	20
2. Live Birth	0
3. Hair or Fur	20
4. Milk Production	20
5. Breaths Oxygen	20
Final Evaluation (Content/Standard)	80

Quality Criteria	Evaluation
1. Follow Directions	20
2. Neat	20
3. Easy to Understand	0
4. Complete	20
5. Personal Best	0
Final Evaluation (Quality)	60

Evaluating Assessments that Contain More Than One Standard

Often, assessments will measure more than one standard. Since the system I am discussing in this book is standards-based, in a case where one assessment measures multiple standards, the standards must be evaluated separately. In the grade book and eventually on the reporting tool, they will be entered standard by standard.

When you plan for an assessment, you are targeting specific standards. You should identify and evaluate those standards when scoring students' assessments. How does that evaluation look on the product itself when there is more than one standard? You list the standards and their respective scores on the product. Or if you use the *Standards-Based Scoring of Formative/Summative Assessments* (Figure 3.13 and Appendix A), complete one form for the assessment. The standards and their evaluations can each be listed on a separate row.

The bottom line is that we are talking about a standards-based system here. Therefore, standards must be assessed and evaluated to reflect such a system. There should be no averaging of different standards scores to make one score. List them separately in and of themselves. Then, record them accordingly into your standards-based grade book.

Checking for Understanding

Formative assessments don't always have to be lengthy, time-consuming assignments or products. They can be quick checks in the middle or at the end of a lesson. They can be quick-writes or symbols. They can be observational or verbal. In any case, these quick checks help you to immediately determine where to take your instruction at that moment.

On-the-Spot Checks

Use these strategies during the teacher-directed instruction part of your lesson. If you see glassy eyes or frustrated brows appear on students' faces, this may be the time to stop and take a moment to check for understanding. You should make a habit of doing this periodically during whole-group instruction as it is a great way to actively involve students on a moment's notice. Make sure you choose strategies that will elicit honest responses. You do not want their responses to be influenced by peers or the worry of being wrong. The following are On-the-Spot strategies for checking for understanding. They include:

- page protectors
- quick check
- personal assessment
- think-pair-share

Page Protectors

Each student has a glossy page protector with a sheet of lined or plain paper inserted inside. The teacher asks a quick question about content, and students draw a symbol or written response on the page with an erasable marker. Students hold up their responses for the teacher to see.

Quick Check

During teacher-directed instruction, the teacher stops every few minutes to ask a quick question or make a statement regarding the content just covered. Students have 4" × 6" cards on their desks marked with *True* and *False* or *Yes* and *No*. Students hold up appropriate cards in response to the teacher's questions or statements right in front of their chests. By raising the cards in this way, responses are somewhat hidden from others around the room so that students can respond without feeling intimidated. All students are responding in the same way at the same time as opposed to asking for agreement or disagreement by the raising of hands. Each student commits to a response in a comfortable, nonthreatening setting.

Personal Assessment

The teacher makes a statement about the content. Students respond to the teacher's question by putting a fist to their chest and indicating agreement or disagreement with a "thumbs up" or a "thumbs down" gesture. The same can be done with fingers. One finger up means *Yes*, two fingers up means *No*. As with the Quick Check, pressing the fist to the chest personalizes the response without being influenced by others' opinions in the class.

Think-Pair-Share

The teacher asks a question about content. Students are given a few seconds to think about the answer, allowing time for processing before sharing. When the time is up, they discuss their answers with partners. The teacher circulates the room, listening for understanding.

Out-the-Door Checks

These checks occur at the end of a lesson or when students are leaving for the day. On-the-Spot checks can work here, although more time can be allowed for Out-the-Door Checks. They are still relatively quick but can require filling in blanks or answering questions in written or symbolic form. In each case, students respond to only one question or one prompt. Filling out multiple boxes or answering too many questions takes too long, which negates the status of "quick check." If it takes too long to complete, students may hurry through and not be thoughtful or sincere in their responses. The following are examples of Out-the-Door strategies for checking for understanding. They include:

- ticket out
- exit cards
- sticky note parking
- making faces
- four corners

Ticket Out

A *Ticket Out* check (Figure 3.14) consists of a simple questions on a grid. Students complete the *Ticket Out* at the end of a lesson and use it as their ticket out the door when exiting the classroom or before transitioning to a new topic, activity, or subject area. This resource can be found in Appendix A.

Figure 3.14 Ticket Out

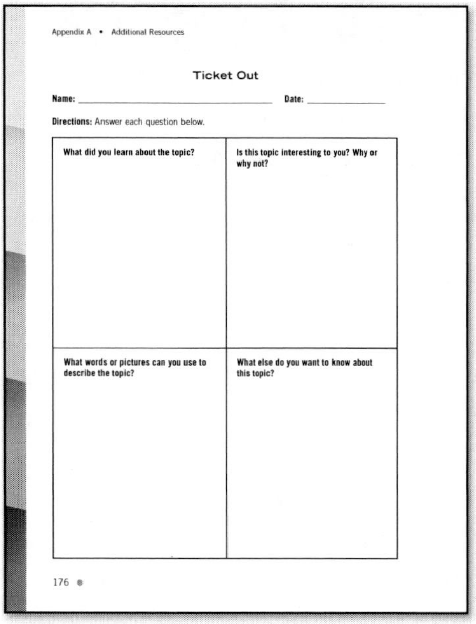
Appendix A • Additional Resources

Ticket Out

Name: ____________________ **Date:** __________

Directions: Answer each question below.

What did you learn about the topic?	**Is this topic interesting to you? Why or why not?**
What words or pictures can you use to describe the topic?	**What else do you want to know about this topic?**

176 •

Exit Cards

Exit Cards (Figure 3.15) are similar to the *Ticket Out* check. *Exit Cards* use shapes, symbols, and text as prompts for reflection on the content of the lesson. This resource can be found in Appendix A.

Sticky Note Parking

On sticky notes, all students will write questions, comments, or responses to a prompt. The teacher designates an area in the room for students to post their sticky notes. The area may be a bulletin board, a space on the wall, a sheet of chart paper on the wall, or on an easel.

Making Faces

The *Making Faces* (Figure 3.16) check uses the symbol of a face to allow students to communicate their answers to the question in a simple format that doesn't require any writing. This resource can be found in Appendix A.

Four Corners

The teacher writes four topics from the unit of study on four posters, one topic on each poster. For example, for a unit on exploration, the names

Figure 3.15 Exit Card

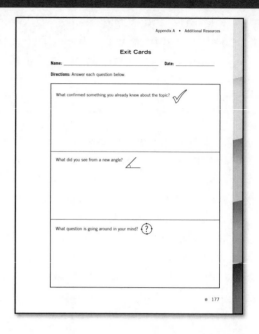

Figure 3.16 Making Faces

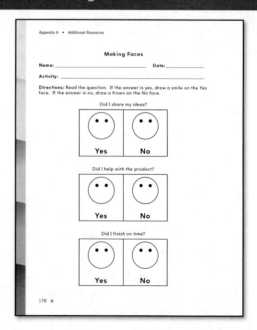

of explorers would be written on each sign: *Columbus, Ponce de Leon, Neil Armstrong,* and *Jacques Cousteau.* The teacher then hangs blank posters at each corner of the classroom. Students are asked to write what they learned about each of the topics on sticky notes, one fact per note, making sure to put their initials on each note. The teacher divides the class into four groups. On the teacher's cue, student groups gather at each of the corners under the poster, one group per corner. Students take turns sharing within their groups what is written on their notes. After they share, they place their notes on the sign. This continues until all students have shared and all notes are on the poster. On the teacher's cue, students rotate clockwise to the next corner, and the process is repeated. This process continues until all groups have visited all four corners.

The information on the notes is not always accurate, and this inevitably becomes part of the discussion when another student in the group sees the error. The teacher continually monitors by visiting the corners as the discussions take place, assessing students' understanding of these key topics. He or she also takes this opportunity to intervene and correct misunderstandings of the topic.

If time does not allow for group discussion in the four corners, the teacher can ask students to simply place their notes on the signs and return to their seats. In either case, the teacher gathers the posters with the sticky notes and can assess understanding of content by what students wrote on their notes.

Using Formative Data to Drive Instruction

Up to this point, we have learned that formative assessments happen as a natural process in the classroom. They are not contrived but occur during the natural flow of daily classroom lessons, and they take on many forms. Now, how do we collect this formative data and record the results so that we can use it to drive future instruction? Since formative assessment *informs*, it is important to use it. This section is dedicated to low-prep, high-impact strategies for collecting and recording formative data in order to plan for future instruction.

Collecting data does not always have to involve complicated checklists and time-consuming paperwork. Formative assessments should not be contrived. Neither should the collection and use of the data. The following are suggestions for doing just that:

- Make Piles
- Use Graphic Organizers

Make Piles

Collecting data can be quick and easy: After you collect in-class assignments or homework and evaluate them, place them in three piles.

- Pile #1—students who still don't get it
- Pile #2—students who are close to mastering the concept
- Pile #3—students who are ready to move on

Now, you have your leveled groups for tomorrow's lesson.

Use Graphic Organizers

You can take the next step after creating these piles by putting the information into a graphic organizer. Figure 3.17 and Figure 3.18 show examples of such an organizer. The first example includes general descriptions for each category; the second is a sample using a science standard. Of course, you will substitute standards and activities to fit your grade level or content area.

Figure 3.17 Prescriptive Differentiation Planning Chart with Descriptions

Prescriptive Differentiation Planning Chart

Standard/Concept: _____
Pre-Assessments: _____

Readiness Levels: (List student names)	Concepts/Skills Known	Prescription
Still Don't Get It!	Vague, if any, understanding of the standard/concept	Learn basic aspects and vocabulary of the standard/concept
Getting There!	Knows most, if not all, aspects of the standard/concept but may not be consistent in accurately demonstrating this understanding	Opportunities to describe and apply all aspects of the standard/concept consistently, including accurate use of vocabulary
Got It!	Knowledgeable about all aspects of the standard/concept and vocabulary. Is consistent in accurately demonstrating this understanding	Apply the standard/concept in depth and complexity, perhaps connecting to real-life situations and problem-solving opportunities

Figure 3.18 Prescriptive Differentiation Planning Chart Sample

Prescriptive Differentiation Planning Chart

Standard/Concept: Describe the Life Cycle of a Butterfly

Pre-Assessments: KWL; draw a picture; verbal question and answer

Readiness Levels: (List student names)	Concepts/Skills Known	Prescription
Still Don't Get It! Jeremy Todd Ginni Peyton Ronald Sheena Gracie Riley	Little experience with the life cycle of a butterfly	Teacher-directed instruction: Learn basic aspects of the life cycle of a butterfly, including all vocabulary
Getting There! Georgia Nina Samuel Pamela Peter Chen Hijun	Knows some, but not all, of the stages of the life cycle of a butterfly Knows some of the vocabulary related to the life cycle of a butterfly	Practice unknown vocabulary connected to the life cycle of a butterfly Opportunities to describe all stages of the life cycle of a butterfly; choose activities from an activities menu
Got It! JaQuez Melissa Armando	Knowledgeable about all aspects of the life cycle of a butterfly Proficient in vocabulary and terms related to the content	Project: Comparison of butterfly life cycle to other life cycles Application: choose in-depth activities from an application menu

The horizontal boxes indicate levels of understanding of the content. Student names are written in the first vertical column. Results of their formative assessments are noted in the second vertical column. Prescription for future learning and instruction are noted in the third vertical column. No need to go into detail here—short notes will do. A blank template of this graphic organizer can be found in Appendix A.

Use Your Grade Book

Now that we've talked about what formative assessment is, how to do it, and how to collect the data, let's talk logistics in terms of storing and organizing that data. Keep a page in your grade book that is designated just for formative assessments. If your grade book is online, check to see if this version has the capacity to separate the formative assessments from the summative. Remember, the formative assessments are for diagnosis and prescriptive purposes and summative assessments are for final reporting. Evaluations of any nature (percentages, points, checks, smiley faces, etc.) are recorded in the grade book for every assessment type. Since formative assessments are practice and occur continually, there should be plenty of room to enter a high volume of assessments. And since the assessments focus on standards, the format of the grade book should show the assessments *and* the standard(s) that are being measured.

Figure 3.19 Formative Grade Book Page Sample

Figure 3.19 is a sample standards-based, formative grade book page for science. Note that there's also a place within each assessment to enter a content score and a product quality score. There's only one row of quality scores listed to avoid confusion when reading this page.

Content Area: Science	Standard/Activity	SCI.2 Solutions/Mixtures Vocab	SCI.2 Mixtures vs. Solutions	SCI.2 Solutions Treasure Hunt	SCI.2 Gases & Liquids Summary	SCI.2 Mixtures & Solutions Quiz	New Standard	SCI.4 Levers & Pulleys Vocab	SCI.4 Why Wedges Work Essay	SCI.4 Wheels & Axles Picture	SCI.4 Machines Invention	SCI.4 Simple Machines Quiz
Students/Quality												
Blevins, Jeremy							X					
Quality							X					
Brown, Betsy		72	62	83	4	93	X	4	79	83		
Quality		4/5	3/5	4/5	2/5	5/5	X	4/5	4/5	5/5		
Carpenter, Mindy							X					
Quality							X					
Dempsey, Paul		55	65	72	3	83	X	3	67	77		
Quality							X					
Huggins, Stephanie		65	70	77	4	83	X	2	56	78		
Quality							X					
Hall, LaKeisha		56	75	88	3	95	X	3	68	85		
Quality							X					
Sweet, Samuel		42	68	73	3	73	X	3	75	73		
Quality							X					
Romero, Manuel		67	72	83	4	85	X	2	59	72		
Quality							X					

Scores should be entered horizontally for each standards-based assessment. At any time, you can look vertically down a column to see if and where future instruction is needed. In the sample, when looking at the results of the first assessment for Standard Science 1.1, the teacher sees that Paul, Samuel, and LaKeisha are still in need of a lot of help (Still Don't Get It!). The teacher will pull those three together for small-group instruction. Betsy, Stephanie, and Manuel seem to be on track at this point in the unit (Getting There!). There is no one so far who has exceeded expectations (Got It!). The common-sense, time-saving rationale to organizing your formative grade book in this way is that your small groups are laid out for you every time you enter a set of scores. A blank template of this resource can be found in Appendix A.

When the line of formative assessment scores on any given standard begins to reveal a distinct pattern of mastery, it's then time to shift the assessment mode from formative to summative. Here, at the crest of the learning curve, students now move from practice to final displays of mastery. Congratulations! Your students have climbed the formative portion of the assessment and evaluation learning curve, reached the crest, and indicated mastery of the concepts. Now it is time to begin the journey through the summative portion of the learning curve.

Review and Reflect

1. How do you communicate that formative assessments are practice to your students?

2. Do your students question the importance of formative assessments when you tell them they are for practice? How do you answer those questions?

3. Think about how formative assessment scores should not be averaged with summative scores on the report card, but rather they should be used to determine student needs for further instruction. What are you doing in your classroom to help students understand this idea?

4. How have you used homework as a formative assessment? What problems do you encounter with homework? Why do you think this happens? How can you use what you've learned about formative assessments to help solve those problems?

4

Summative Assessments

"Institutional assessment efforts should not be concerned about valuing what can be measured but instead, about measuring that which is valued."
—T. W. Banta et al. (1996)

What Are Summative Assessments?

Summative assessments are purposeful activities assigned to students when they have completed their journey up the learning curve and are now sitting at the top, ready for the chance to demonstrate mastery of content. Summative assessments are not like formative assessments, which are designed to provide the immediate, explicit feedback useful for helping teachers and students during the learning process. In contrast, summative assessments are used to measure student growth after instruction and are generally administered at the end of a unit in order to determine whether long-term learning goals have been met (Coffey 2009). Summative data can shape how teachers organize their curriculum or shape what courses schools offer their students (FairTest: The National Center for Fair & Open Testing 2008).

Summative assessments can take on many forms. Anything your students say and anything they do can be utilized as summative assessment if the data collected is being used to demonstrate a final show of mastery. Use your common sense to decide when to record and report these items as summative assessment. This chapter will help you understand how to do this.

Planning Activities for Summative Assessment

When planning for summative assessments, apply the same criteria discussed in Chapter 3. Summative assessments:

- are natural, not contrived
- are open-ended whenever possible
- incorporate a range of standards in the content area and/or are cross-curricular
- are relevant and developmentally appropriate
- reflect the many ways in which students learn

Plan your activities for summative assessment in accordance with what you are trying to measure for mastery—that is, your state or district standards. As was the case with formative assessment, you can use the list of student-created products (see Chapter 3) to make menus and checklists for students to choose from. The only difference now is that these product evaluations, or scores, will be recorded in a grade book for summative assessments. And as I will explain in Chapter 5, these evaluations and scores should be those that show up on the student's final report card.

How Often and How Many Summative Assessments Should Be Given?

Since summative assessments are given at the end of a unit of study, the number given will be fewer than that of formative assessments, which are given on an ongoing basis during the course of everyday instruction within the unit. The number will depend on the depth and complexity of the unit itself. For example, a shorter unit on the life cycle of plants may require fewer summative assessments than, say, a unit on the causes and effects of the Civil War. In either case, more than one summative assessment should be given at the end of a unit. The formats should differ each time in order to give every student the opportunity to show understanding in a variety of ways in order to accommodate their learning profiles. According to Robert Marzano's research (2000), "Students must be given more than one opportunity to show their new level of understanding." His research also tells us that "short, frequent assessments are more effective than long, infrequent ones." What does this mean for summative assessment? This means that summative assessments should be given in a variety of forms and as frequently as is appropriate to the scope and sequence of your curriculum.

Summative Assessments Can Take on Many Forms

Assessment is not a synonym for testing. My experience in working in schools across the nation has been that many teachers equate assessments with tests and quizzes. Quizzes are given throughout the course of the unit, and tests are given at the end. However, these are only two forms of assessment. There are many others! Assessment is gathering data, so everything students say and do (e.g., assignments, activities, products, and/or behaviors) can be considered for summative assessment purposes. What *form* the assessment takes does not determine whether it is summative or formative. It is *when* the assessment occurs that determines the type. In other words, when assessments in any form occur before a unit begins, they are *pre-assessments*. When they occur during the course of the unit, they are *formative assessments*. When they occur at the end of a unit of study, they are *summative*.

Since every job or career yields different types of products, integrate this scenario into your class routine by letting students experience a vast selection of products to use as summative assessments rather than relying heavily on just one form, such as paper-pencil. We will now explore several different forms of summative assessment. These include:

- Paper-Pencil Assessment

- Project-Based Assessment

- Problem-Based Assessment

Paper-Pencil Assessments

One form often used for summative assessment more so than for formative assessment is the paper-pencil assessment type, which includes fill-in-the-blank, matching, multiple-choice, modified multiple choice (in which the student writes an explanation for his or her answer), short answer (one- or two-sentence response), or essay (extended written response). Teachers sometimes use these types of paper-pencil assessments because they are provided with their textbooks or other teaching materials, or because other teachers in their subject or grade level have decided to use the same assessments among themselves in order to ensure continuity and standardization across grades or content areas.

Although there are benefits to using paper-pencil assessment for summative purposes, they should be used only periodically, not exclusively. You should also be incorporating authentic forms of assessments, including observational assessments, as well as student-created products, such as comic strips, illustrations, games, models, or any other items (see Figure 3.1) . The goal is to avoid relying on any one form of assessment. Keep assessments authentic in order to stay in alignment with the learning modalities of your students.

Figure 4.1 shows varying forms of written assessments. It also includes performance-based assessment in order to show how this type of assessment compares with the other forms with regard to higher-order thinking skills. The chart shows which forms of assessment are effective in assessing deeper levels of understanding (i.e., what a student *really* knows about the content). When a student taps into higher-order thinking skills in order to respond to a prompt, he or she is likely showing deeper conceptual understanding by making connections through application of content as opposed to recall, which is based on short-term retention.

Figure 4.1 Assessment Tools and Levels of Thinking

	Retention	Micro Thinking	Higher-Order Thinking Skills		
			Critical Thinking	Creative Thinking	Problem Solving/ Decision Making
Fill in the Blank	X				
Matching	X	X			
Multiple Choice	X	X			
Modified Multiple Choice		X	X		
Short Answer		X	X	X	X
Essay			X	X	X
Performance-Based			X	X	X

Assessment Tools and Levels of Thinking

The type of assessment we choose is governed by the level of thinking we wish to measure. Conversely, the level of thinking we wish to measure governs the type of assessment we choose.

As illustrated by Figure 4.1, the assessment types that lend themselves most readily to higher-order thinking skills are short answer, essay, and performance-based. The following are examples for each category, including short-answer responses to open-ended questions; written essays, which are longer, more in-depth answers to open-ended questions; and performance-based assessments. You should note that all directions are tied directly to curriculum standards. When creating these assessment types for your class, remember to focus on your standards, and then assess!

Short Answer

Short answer assessments include one- to two-sentence or short paragraph answers to open-ended questions. Examples include:

- Describe the life cycle of a plant.
- Describe the process for finding the area of a square.
- Name three community workers and describe their jobs.

Essay

Essay assessments are multiparagraph written responses to open-ended questions. Unlike short answer responses, essays are more in-depth and usually require examples and support. Essays are considered a type of performance-based assessment. Examples include:

- Describe the life cycle of a plant. Explain how drought, flooding, or fire can affect the life cycle. Include examples.

- Describe the process of how to find the area of a square and how this process can be used in our everyday lives.

- Name three community workers and describe their jobs. Explain how these workers help people in the community.

Performance-Based

Performance-based assessments require students to demonstrate their knowledge or skills. One key feature is that they require students to be active participants. They also focus attention on how students arrive at their answers and require them to demonstrate the knowledge or skills needed to obtain a correct answer. Examples include:

- Projects that enable students to work on a complex problem and require planning, research, internal discussion, and a final presentation.

- Essays assessing students' understanding of content through a written description, an analysis, an explanation, or a summary.

- Experiments assessing how well students understand scientific concepts and can carry out scientific processes.

- Demonstrations that give students opportunities to show mastery of standards-based content and procedures.

- Portfolios that allow students to provide a broad portrait of their performance through files that contain collections of students' work, assembled over time.

Yes, it's true that so much depends on the one high-stakes test students in grades two and higher are given once a year, which usually comes in the multiple-choice, bubble-in-the-answer format. This has been the case for decades. According to Figure 4.1, the levels of thinking required by the student to complete many of these assessments lie in the "short-term retention" category. Even though the scientific method, which is the underlying process for producing valid data, and common sense belies the validity of staking so much on the results of just one test, we are mandated to do so. So in all fairness to your students and in the interest of providing a variety of assessments, be sure to interject a multiple-choice, bubble-in-the-answer test here and there. This will ensure that your students at least are given the opportunity to practice taking those types of tests. I also recommend that you change those multiple-choice formats to modified multiple choice. This means that for every bubbled in or circled answer, the student must write a brief explanation as to why they made that choice.

The recommendation is simple: maintain a good balance of assessment choices to accommodate the multiple intelligences of your students. The whole point of summative assessments is to determine if your students understand the information. Give them several opportunities to show their understanding of the same content in different ways.

Project-Based Assessment

Perhaps the word *project* strikes terror in your heart. I imagine you immediately think of the hours of planning, the gathering of materials, the chaos in the classroom, the hours (if not days) of precious classroom time used up, and the confusion over how to grade fairly. Then there's the vision of the parent who does the project for the student or the dreaded call from another parent who is certain, if the project was a group effort, that his or her child did all the work and everyone else got credit for it.

Project-based assessment is a format that involves students in complex, in-depth study. The goal of project-based assessment is to have students show their comprehension of the standards in a unit of study by completing a series of steps that leads to the creation of a project. Projects give students opportunities to apply what they are learning at different readiness levels, interests, and learning modalities.

Although it's true that summative assessments take on many of the same forms as formative assessments, there are some that are exclusive to the summative category. Projects typically fall into this category, though they can also be used formatively when students are still practicing and the unit is nearing its end.

Projects are important, as this form of assessment truly mirrors what goes on in the real world. Howard Gardner of the Multiple Intelligences Theory says, "Most of what you do in life is a project" (1983). Think about that. I challenge you to name anything you do throughout your day that is not a project in some shape or form. Doing the laundry. Paying bills. Cleaning the house. Planning a vacation. In just about everything we do, every day, there's planning. We think about the steps to take and the resources and materials to gather in order to complete the task. Classroom projects require that same intensity of planning. The student—or students, if it's a group project—must make many decisions. What is the unit of study? What standards-based content needs to be demonstrated in the project? Who will participate? What are the products necessary for completion of the project? How will the content and products be delegated? What materials are needed? Where can the materials be found? How will the research be conducted? What is the timeline for completion? How will the project be shared or presented? Class projects effectively prepare students for what they will encounter in the world outside the classroom, so use them as frequently as time allows.

What makes projects valuable as summative assessments? Because projects involve application of content through steps, procedures, and active participation, students are provided with the opportunity to demonstrate their understanding of all the content and standards that make up the unit. This is performance-based assessment at its finest! Projects require higher levels of thinking as students work to discover the big picture as it relates to the topic and how all the standards fit together into one neat package that defines the unit of study.

Please note that projects should not be the only summative assessment at the end of a unit of study. (See the other forms of summative assessments described previously.) As I have pointed out many times in this book, various other forms of summative assessments need to be assigned as well. Students need to have more than one opportunity to show their levels of understanding. Since projects are so time intensive, interjecting various short forms of summative assessments is appropriate as well. For example, short-answer, ticket-out, or short multiple-choice responses can all be used in conjunction with a project. Also, projects do not have to be required for every unit of study because they do take time. Simply be realistic and assign them as often as possible.

The following key questions and step-by-step planning guide should provide some structure for implementing project-based assessments and make them seem less overwhelming.

Key Questions for Planning Projects

Projects can take many forms, such as products, presentations, and/ or performances. When creating your plan for project-based assessment, consider the following:

1. Is the project devoted only to a single subject area, or is there a connection to other content areas?

2. Is the project tied to content-area standards for the unit?

3. Can materials and resources for the planning of the project be found within the walls of the classroom (e.g., teacher resources, student activity ideas, means for evaluation)?

4. Can all students in your class participate? Projects should not be reserved for your accelerated or high-ability students, as all students should be able to participate.

5. Is there ample time for project completion?

6. Is the project collaborative? If so, is the collaboration with persons outside the school or within a classroom setting? Such collaboration will take more time, as will monitoring collaboration to help students learn how to be a part of a team and communicate appropriately with others.

7. Is there an opportunity for students to benefit both academically and personally from their involvement in the project? Consider that when students interact with other students and experts across the country or internationally, they get a broader feel for diversity. Their participation in a real-world activity might encourage them to do their best work and see the relevance of the content-area concepts in their daily lives.

8. Do students have a choice in the selection of different aspects of the standards-based unit? For example, if the unit is on the solar system, do they have choices as to which planets they want to do their projects on? The teacher can provide these choices while still ensuring that all planets are covered collectively as a class. Alternatively, if students are to do a project on all the standards of the unit, are they given choices on how they want to depict what they know? This is where a product menu comes in handy. When students have input, they tend to become more involved and excited about the project.

9. Is there a monetary cost involved in the creation of the project? Create rules and criteria so that there will be no surprises when it comes time for the gathering of materials. Students will need to plan accordingly.

—Adapted from Ashley Brooks (2004)

Project Planning Step-by-Step

After you consider the key questions, take the following steps to help plan and execute a project for your class.

Step 1: Identify the Unit of Study and Standards-Based Content

Identify the unit of study for the project. For project-based assessment, you provide the unit of study and students are then responsible for identifying the standards that make up that unit. The content standards that are tied to that unit are what will be assessed and evaluated. All of these standards must be represented in the products that the students create for the project. For example, if you provide the unit of study "Characteristics of Mammals" in your science class, students are responsible for identifying the various characteristics of mammals (e.g., has fur or hair and breathes oxygen) and including this content in their projects. Students' ability to identify and demonstrate understanding of the standards in their projects is how you assess their mastery of the standards.

Step 2: Plan the Project

After students are aware of the standards/content that must be included in their projects, provide them with a menu of products. See Figure 3.1 for a list of products that could be included on the menu. Each student will choose from this menu to develop the individual products that will make up the project. You may want to give students a required number of products to complete for the project (e.g., if it's a group project, the number can be based on the number of students in each group). Most importantly, however, students will plan how to include the content within the various products. For instance, in the "Characteristics of Mammals" example from Step 1, if a student identifies that there are five characteristics of mammals and he or she is required to create three products for a project, the student must plan what pieces of the content (i.e., which characteristics) they will represent in each of the three products. When the individual products are combined to form the larger project, thus combining the pieces of the content, the resulting project reflects all of the standards-based content. See Figure 4.2 to see how this can be done.

Along with deciding which parts of the content will be targeted with each product, students decide who is responsible for each part of the content and the product that will show that content in a group-project scenario. Whether students are completing projects individually or in groups, they also need to identify the materials needed and develop a timeline for completion. The timeline may come from you.

All the planning can be written in the form of a project plan or contract. The project plan should detail the *what*, *who*, and *when* of the project.

Step 3: Complete the Project

Students pursue research on the content of the unit of study and create products that will depict their understanding of the content. The teacher monitors their progress by assisting with resources, checking for on-task behavior, and assuring that their focus remains on the content. Projects should be evaluated halfway through for possible revisions in the process.

Step 4: Collaborate on Content

Group projects provide the time for students to review the parts of the standards/content included in one another's products. All group members should collaborate to ensure accuracy of the content. Students should also rehearse the final presentation, if applicable.

It is important to hold students accountable for this step. For example, in Figure 4.4, each member of the group is required to confirm their review of the content produced by the other group members. They do so by initialing beside each product on the plan. A blank template of this resource can be found in Appendix A.

Students should use content- and quality-criteria checklists to evaluate the final project before turning it in to the teacher. This allows students the opportunity to make necessary revisions before a final grade is assigned.

Step 5: Presentation

Projects are then submitted for final evaluation and presented at a predetermined time. Remember that the presentation of the projects can be done in a variety of ways. Students can display their projects in an exhibit-style for others to view, they can give formal presentations of their projects to the rest of the class, or they can give an informal presentation of their project to you only. The evaluation of the final version of the project is what is entered into the summative grade book.

Step 6: Evaluate the Process

Students reflect on and evaluate the process when all is said and done. What went right or wrong? How could I improve next time? This reflection gives students goals to work toward in future project-based assessments.

Figures 4.2, 4.3, and 4.4 show examples of a variety of project planning menus. Completed project plans become project contracts. In Figure 4.2, the content and products are categorized into multiple intelligences groups. An example of a product in the visual/spatial category may be to create a poster or a diagram. A product in the musical/rhythmical category may be to write lyrics to a song. You can create a menu of products sorted by intelligence group for students to choose from as they complete their project plans. The boxes are checked as the products are completed. A blank template of this resource can be found in Appendix A.

Figure 4.2 Sample Intelligences Project Planning Menu

Intelligences Project Planning Menu

Name(s): Belinda Stephens

Unit of Study: Characteristics of Mammals

Date: 10/10/2012 **Goal Date for Completion:** 10/20/2012

Standards/Content: Characteristics of Mammals: fur/hair, gives milk, breathes oxygen, live birth, warm blooded

- ❑ **Verbal/Linguistic Product:** write a poem
  Content: warm blooded
- ❑ **Logical/Mathematical Product:** ____
  Content: ____
- ❑ **Visual/Spatial Product:** create a diagram
  Content: fur/hair and breathes oxygen
- ❑ **Bodily/Kinesthetic Product:** ____
  Content: ____
- ❑ **Musical/Rhythmical Product:** write and perform a rap
  Content: live birth and gives milk
- ❑ **Naturalist/Environmental Product:** ____
  Content: ____
- ❑ **Interpersonal Product:** ____
  Content: ____
- ❑ **Intrapersonal Product:** ____
  Content: ____

Materials / Resources Needed: with pen, paper, computer with word processing, graphic organizer template, magazines with pictures of mammals to cut out for graphic organizer, MP3/CD player with rap beat for rap performance

Figure 4.3 is an *Individual Project Planning Menu.* It is intended for individual projects only. The student lists the standards/content of the unit that has been designated by the teacher and the products that will be created to depict the content. This menu differs from the *Intelligences Project Planning Menu* because the products on the *Individual Project Planning Menu* may or may not be based on multiple intelligences. The product choices on this menu can be based on other criteria, such as student interests or preferred learning styles. The important thing is simply to make sure that students have a variety of choices to show what they know. For example, for a unit on explorers in the New World, allow students to choose the explorer and then offer a variety of product choices. Students then choose three products and tie each product to the content that they are to show within the project. For example, a student's selected explorer, possible products, and content are shown below. The content is underlined and the product is italicized:

Figure 4.3 Individual Project Planning Menu

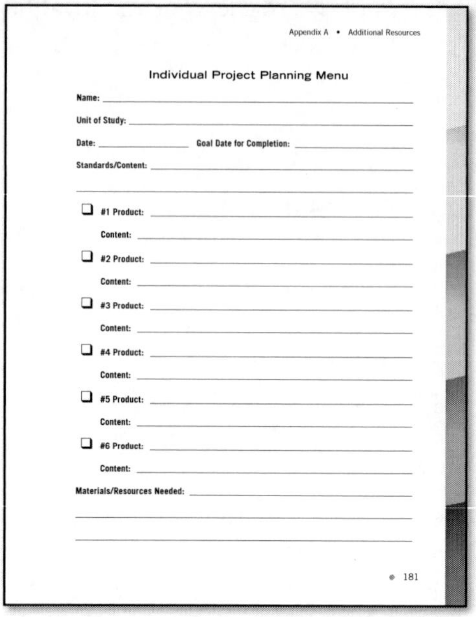

Appendix A • Additional Resources

Individual Project Planning Menu

Name: __________

Unit of Study: __________

Date: __________ Goal Date for Completion: __________

Standards/Content: __________

- ❑ #1 Product: __________
  Content: __________
- ❑ #2 Product: __________
  Content: __________
- ❑ #3 Product: __________
  Content: __________
- ❑ #4 Product: __________
  Content: __________
- ❑ #5 Product: __________
  Content: __________
- ❑ #6 Product: __________
  Content: __________

Materials/Resources Needed: __________

181

Product #1: As Christopher Columbus, write a *letter* to a friend detailing your discoveries, travels, and hardships.

Product #2: Make a *color poster* depicting the routes Christopher Columbus took.

Product #3: Create a *3D model* of the products acquired on the voyages of Christopher Columbus. Include an explanation as to why these products were valuable.

A blank template of this resource can be found in Appendix A.

When the project is a group effort, the *Group Project Plan* (Figure 4.4) is an effective format. The content and products are listed and delegated, with a checkbox that the assigned group member uses to indicate completion of the product. Individual accountability is the focus of the checkbox. Beside the space for each product is a box for the other group members to place their initials. Initialing this box indicates that the student has reviewed the content of this product and has collaborated with the other group members on its accuracy. Group accountability for the content in the project is the focus of this box.

As you can see by the example, the key difference between the individual and the group projects is that the content/products are delegated among a group of people rather than having one person do it all. A blank template of this resource can be found in Appendix A.

Evaluating Projects

How you evaluate a project sets the tone for planning and collaboration. Therefore, students must know up front how they will be evaluated and held accountable for showing what they know, whether it is a group project or an individual project.

Figure 4.4 Group Project Plan

Group Project Plan

Names: Belinda, Jeremy, Rudi, Yolanda

Unit of Study: Characteristics of Mammals Group Project

Standards/Content: Characteristics of Mammals: fur or hair, gives milk, breathes oxygen, live birth, warm blooded

Date: 10/10/12 **Goal Date for Completion:** 10/24/12

	Review by group (Initial here)
☐ **#1 Product:** write a poem **Content:** live birth and gives milk **Group Member Assigned:** Yolanda	JY
☐ **#2 Product:** create a diagram depicting the characteristic **Content:** breathes oxygen **Group Member Assigned:** Jeremy	YC
☐ **#3 Product:** build a 3D model depicting the characteristic **Content:** fur or hair **Group Member Assigned:** Rudi	RL
☐ **#4 Product:** record a mammal interview about the characteristic **Content:** warm-blooded **Group Member Assigned:** Belinda	BY

Materials/Resources Needed: paper, pencils, marker, scissors, items for 3-D model (cardboard, Styrofoam, fake fur or fabric), glue, Internet and books for research

Let's start with the big picture. Projects are one product made up of many parts. The whole equals the sum of its parts. Therefore, the project receives one score for content, no matter if it is a project completed by an individual or by a group. And as with any assessment, you can also give the project a separate score for quality.

The only difference between an individual project and a group project is that with the group plan, the content and products are delegated, and with the individual plan, the content and products are completed by one person. In both cases, there is a group of standards-based content and products that, when put together, make up the whole project.

Often, teachers may give an individual project one score, making sure that the total possible points for each component of the project add up to 100 percent. Yet with a group project, each student in the group may receive an individual grade of up to 100 percent just for his or her own task. In this case, a project consisting of four products completed individually by four students could receive a total score of 400 percent. When a project is handled this way, students are really working on individual assignments and they just happen to be sitting together in a group, perhaps consulting with one another. These are four separate assignments, not one project.

A project is a sum of its parts no matter if there is one person or many people contributing to it. With a group project, how does that idea transfer to the evaluation in a summative grade book? Each student as a cooperating member of the group receives the project's final grade.

To establish the common-sense perspective of this practice, let me give you an example of how this works in the world outside the classroom. A good friend of mine is a mechanical engineer and works with a team to develop medical instruments. The members of the team each have a job to do in the creation of a new instrument. In the end, the instrument is evaluated as a whole, and the group receives feedback and recognition for the creation of this one tool. If someone in the team slacks off, the instruments' quality is affected and the whole team is held accountable and responsible. That is the nature of a collaborative project.

Figure 4.5 shows a graphic depiction of project evaluation as I have described it. One project equals one grade no matter how the parts were delegated. The pieces of the content and the products are the parts of the whole project.

Figure 4.5 Graphic Model of Evaluation

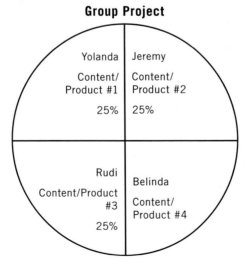

Individual Project

Me Content/ Product #1 25%	Me Content/ Product #2 25%
Me Content/Product #3 25%	Me Content/Product #4 25%

Group Project

Yolanda Content/ Product #1 25%	Jeremy Content/ Product #2 25%
Rudi Content/Product #3 25%	Belinda Content/ Product #4

Content/Product #1 + Content/Product #2 + Content/Product #3 + Content/Product #4 = One Project

Highest Possible Score: 100%

Assigning one grade for a group project may be a giant step for you at this point. Perhaps you would prefer to start by assigning individual projects. Remember, though, that your classroom is an excellent place to prepare your students for how they will be treated in the workplace, and group projects are an effective way to do this. And when you decide to assign group projects, students can make comparisons to what was involved when they completed individual projects. They can see how delegation of responsibility lightens their load as opposed to doing all the work themselves. Plus, when they work collaboratively, they have the opportunity to check their understanding of the content with their group members and work together to make the project the best it can be.

Also, be aware that you don't have to switch one project structure for another (i.e., start with only individual projects and then move to only group projects). You can do both. Sometimes you may want to assign group projects, and other times you may want students to work individually. Sometimes you may want to give them choices on whether to work individually, in a group, or with a partner. Offering choices gains student buy-in, which begets motivation and active participation!

Self- and Peer-Evaluations

Self- and peer-evaluations provide students with opportunities for reflection and solid recommendations for improvement. Students can evaluate their own performances as well as the performances of their peers if the project is a group effort. The teacher can also use these student evaluations to see who needs help with organization, research, and collaboration skills. This information can provide insight for the teacher and the student on how to improve project planning

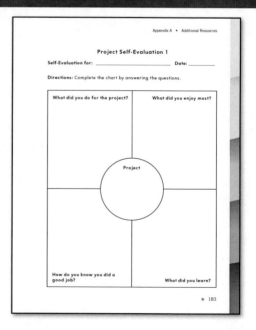

Figure 4.6 Project Self-Evaluation 1

and creation of projects in the future. Figures 4.6 and 4.7 are examples of project self- and peer-evaluations. Figure 4.6 is meant for younger students. Figure 4.7 is meant for older students. These resources can be found in Appendix A.

Group Participation Evaluation

The evaluations shown in Figures 4.8 and 4.9 are meant for group projects. Have students complete the appropriate evaluation by doing the following:

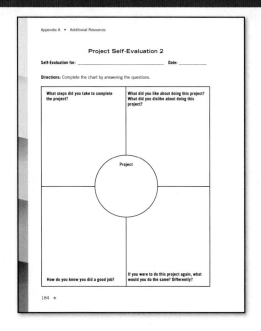

Figure 4.7 Project Self-Evaluation 2

- Make copies of the evaluation form for students.

- Have each group member complete an evaluation form.

- Instruct students to pass their form to the rest of the group members until everyone has evaluated every other student in the group. The evaluations should then be reviewed by the group for discussion and feedback purposes.

Completed evaluations are returned to the teacher for review. Then, they are either attached to the project itself or included in the students' unit portfolios.

Participation Evaluation 1 (Figure 4.8), does not evaluate others but rather the students' own perception of how they contributed to the group project. *Note:* This could also be used for individual projects as well. Figure 4.9, *Participation Evaluation 2*, is meant for older students. Use your judgment on the developmental appropriateness of this format. These resources can be found in Appendix A.

Problem-Based Assessment

Problem-based assessment measures the highest levels of thinking. Sometimes referred to as problem-based learning, it requires critical thinking, creativity, and of course, problem solving. These three areas ensure that the student is using every bit of his or her knowledge and understanding of the content to reach a goal. This type of assessment is performance-based and may be used less frequently than project-based assessment simply because of the sheer nature of it. Problem-based assessment can occur more than once as a summative assessment for a unit, so it can be more time-consuming. But remember, you can assess

Figure 4.8 Participation Evaluation 1

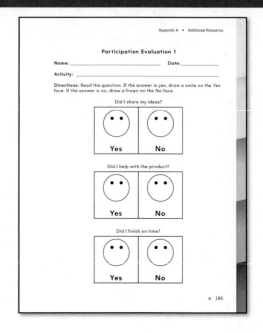

Figure 4.9 Participation Evaluation 2

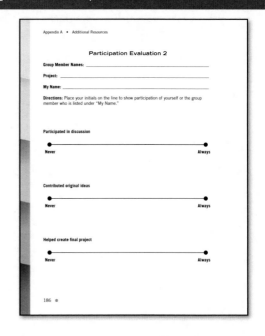

numerous standards all at once. And while the student is involved in this problem-solving process, you can use other pieces of information as forms of assessment as well. Examples include assessment of verbal information (e.g., listening to what students say about the content); written information (e.g., a student composes a summation of his or her findings); and variations of the final product (e.g., how students show the final solution to the problem).

What Does It Look Like?

This form of assessment consists of providing students with problems that are open-ended and challenging. Unlike project-based assessment, which has a set of rules and processes to follow, this format is unstructured and extremely open-ended. Students use information and processes in real-world situations to solve the problems. These problems are loosely structured and have no single right answer. They require investigation of options and application of content that students are studying and practicing.

Problem-based assessment requires a combination of the following components, which have been adapted from Gallagher, Rosenthal, and Stepien (1993):

1. **Reliance on problems to assess understanding of curriculum standards.** The problems assist in showing the development of targeted standard(s).

2. **The problems are loosely structured.** There is not meant to be one ultimate solution, and as new information is gathered, perception of the problem and thus the solution change.

3. **Students are only given guidelines for approaching the problems.** There is no set formula for solving the problem.

Why Do It?

Problem-based assessment provides the brain with conditions that intrigue and engage. It provides learners with creative opportunities to use their skills in a variety of ways, use a range of resources, and balance their choice of learning with teacher-directed objectives. As Tomlinson and Kalbfleisch (1998) put it, "the brain learns best when it 'does,' rather than when it 'absorbs' [Pally 1997]. Thus, all students must think at a high level to solve knotty problems and to transform the ideas and information they encounter." The ability to access information and use it practically and creatively is a worthy goal because it is useful throughout life.

How Does the Teacher Plan?

The teacher's task is relatively simple. Since the problems are loosely structured and students create their system for solving the problem, this leaves the teacher with these three basic tasks in planning for a problem-based assessment:

1. **Identify all key standards** that will be applied and measured in the assessment.

2. **Clarify the problem.** Make sure all aspects of the problem are understood by students before they begin.

3. **Inform students about how they will be evaluated.** Points? Rubrics?

Figure 4.10, *Problem-Based Assessment Topic Ideas,* provides topic ideas. Modify these to fit your content-area(s) and the grade level(s) you teach. These topics can be written on index cards and stored in an index box for easy student access and future use. Keep in mind that this is a summative assessment, so of course, the topic you choose for students must be connected to the unit of study. The student may also be given the opportunity to brainstorm and choose a topic he or she is excited about as long as it is under the umbrella of the unit content and will give them an opportunity to demonstrate mastery of the standard(s). Remember to keep the focus on the standards, for you are measuring the student against those standards in this assessment. Focus on the standard, then assess!

Math

You are the supervisor of transportation for a local school district. A teacher has asked you if it would be possible to take his or her class on a field trip to the city aquarium. In your response to the teacher, you must include key information crucial to calculating the total cost of the transportation, as well as district budget restrictions.

Social Studies

You are the student council president at your school. Among other things, your school has always been active in community relations. You discover that a popular park near your school is going to close because it costs too much to maintain. You realize that you and your fellow student council members stand a good chance of ensuring that the park can stay open. Design the campaign that can save the park, including how you will work with different members of the city government during the campaign.

Science

You are a geologist, and your area of expertise is the movement of the plates that make up Earth's crust. You understand that the area in which you live is conducive to earthquake activity. Your community is notorious for its apathy and indifference toward the subject of earthquakes. What steps can you take to alert the local population of the dangers of earthquakes and their history in your region so that they may take action should such an event take place?

Language Arts

As an advisor to the president of the United States, you are responsible for reviewing all candidates for the position of U.S. ambassador to Africa. Write the final report you give to the president for your choice for the top nominee, summarizing why you think this candidate will do a good job based on criteria and background that are deemed important for this position.

—Adapted from Ruth Culham and Amanda Wheeler (2003)

How Does the Student Plan?

Students take the following steps in approaching a problem-based assessment. Each step takes time for proper preparation, assimilation, involvement, and development of the outcomes:

1. **Clarify the problem.** Students articulate a problem statement that has been provided by the teacher.

2. **Begin with what you know.** Students should ask themselves, "What do I already know about this problem?" They should examine resources and information that they know from past experiences.

3. **Plan your own approach.** Students should ask themselves, "What do I need to solve this problem? What will I do to get what I need?"

4. **Work at your own pace.** Students generate contracts to manage time and tasks.

5. **Use creative solutions.** Solutions to the problem are presented with backup rationale.

Management During Problem-Based Assessment

How do you help students stay on-task and remain focused within the loosely structured format of problem-based assessment? Simply because a student is ready to take on a problem-based assessment doesn't necessarily mean that he or she is an independent learner. Problem-based assessments (and even project-based, for that matter) require significant amounts of autonomy. The need to work alone comes up often as students conduct research outside the classroom in other areas of the school or even the community. The best way to help a student learn this type of independence is by supporting him or her with paperwork in the form of plans, daily logs, and contracts.

Figure 4.11 Problem-Based Assessment Plan

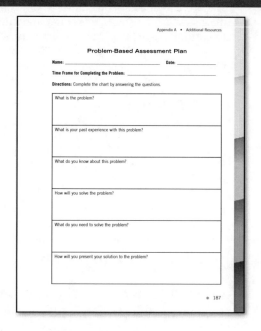

Figure 4.11, *Problem-Based Assessment Plan*, can double as a contract. The assessment plan provides a guide, which is created by students themselves by breaking down the problem-solving process into a sequential format. Retain the plans in your records just as you would any contract. The plans are an

integral part of the finished product. Inclusion of the plan and even the daily log (which will be introduced shortly) shows the process by which the assessment was completed. This resource can be found in Appendix A.

Daily and Weekly Logs

It is crucial that students monitor their progress on a daily and/or weekly basis. This helps them see how they have spent their time and whether they need to revise their plan as the allotted assessment time approaches. The log also holds students accountable for how they have spent their time. Figures 4.12 and 4.13 are examples of such logs for older and younger students, respectively.

Figure 4.12 is a daily log for older students. On the days that students work on their projects, they fill out the log with what they accomplished. This log will be used for the duration of the assessment process. Students can continue on another sheet if need be. This resource can be found in Appendix A.

Figure 4.12 Daily Log

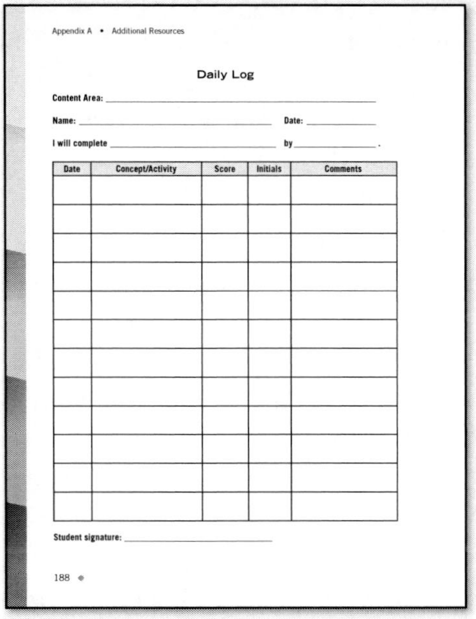

Figure 4.13 Weekly Log

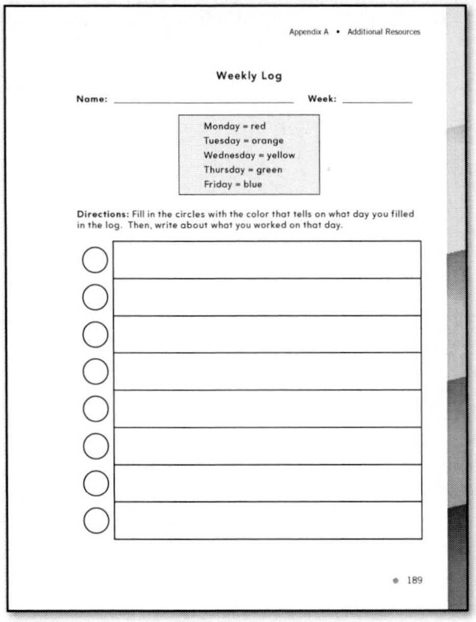

Figure 4.13 is a weekly log for younger students. This log is turned in weekly as opposed to the indefinite time frame for older students. Younger students' problem-based assessments would typically be completed within a week's time, as is developmentally appropriate. As with older students, younger students complete their logs on the days that they work on their projects. They write about what they accomplished and then color the circle to depict the day the log was completed. This resource can be found in Appendix A.

Managing the Paperwork

Managing the paperwork can be summed up in one word: *folders*. You can never have too many folders in your classroom! These folders will hold every aspect of the problem-based assessment, giving details of progress every step of the way. The folder can be transformed into a portfolio to be turned in with the product as part of the summative assessment.

The student always brings the plans and the logs to the table when it is time to confer on progress. Keep in mind that it is crucial that you plan a schedule for when these conferences will take place. All of these procedures will turn even the most distracted student into a goal-setting, on-task learner!

Evaluating Problem-Based Assessments

As for any and all types of assessments, you are measuring the students against the standards that you have targeted for the unit being assessed. The *Problem-Based Assessment Plan* (see Figure 4.11) asks teachers to identify the the standards for the unit that will be measured for the final evaluation. The students were made aware of these expectations as they completed their student plans. When standards and expectations are made clear to students, they can plan and deliver with that standards-based goal in mind.

With that concise list of standards, you can assign points or rubrics to each standard that shows up in students' problem-based assessment activities. Final scores, then, are calculated and reported accordingly.

Presentations

When all is said and done, problem-based assessments can be collected for evaluation and reporting purposes. I strongly suggest, however, that you give students the opportunity to share their hard work with other students, and have them do so *after* the assessments have been evaluated by you. You want to make sure students are sharing accurate information with their peers, so evaluating their assessments beforehand allows students time to revise areas that were incorrect before sharing them in a presentation.

Using Your Grade Book

In Chapter 3, we discussed that evaluations (i.e., scores) of formative assessments should be stored in a grade book or section of a grade book designated for formative assessment. Summative assessments should be recorded in a separate grade book or section of the grade book. This section will look quite different as these scores will be transferred onto the final report card.

Now you have reached the crest of the assessment learning curve. You have learned that summative assessments come in different forms and that students should be given more than one opportunity and more than one way to show their new levels of understanding of content. You've learned that, whenever possible, students should be given the chance to choose how they will show their understanding of content. This ensures a brain-compatible match with how each student's brain processes and reflects. Now we are ready to take a closer look at how to evaluate and report all of this assessment data in a way that makes sense.

Review and Reflect

1. What types of summative assessments have you used? How has that worked for you?

2. Which types of summative assessments have given you the most accurate picture of what students have learned? Why do you think these types of assessments did so?

3. Think about your experiences with assigning projects in your classroom. Describe your positive experiences. Describe your frustrations, if any. What information from this chapter can you use that will help make assigning projects run more smoothly?

5

Final Grading and Reporting

"What makes a child gifted and talented may not always be good grades in school, but a different way of looking at the world and learning."
—Chuck Grassley (2005)

Grade to Show Growth

Here we are at the journey's end as we sit atop the assessment and evaluation learning curve. Pre-assessments have given us enough information to make learning relevant for our students. Formative assessments have driven our instruction. Summative assessments have put the lid on students' practice and have provided evidence that students have reached mastery of content, or at least achieved their personal goals for success.

Now it is time to discuss final grading and reporting of these achievements and to address appropriate grading and reporting tactics. Element #5 of the 5 Essential Elements of differentiated instruction (see Chapter 1) sums it up nicely:

Grade (and report) to show growth.

A student's grade should reflect that student's mastery of grade-level standards, objectives, or benchmarks. Students are measured against the standards, not other students. In turn, these grades are tracked and reported in a way that indicates students' growth and progress over time.

Percentages, Points, Extra Credit, and Weighted Scores

It matters little which form of evaluation you choose to use on summative assessments (e.g., percentages, points, or rubrics). What matters is how the student measures up against the standards that are linked to the assessments. The type of assessment may lend itself to the type of evaluation you use. For example, projects may best be scored with points. Percentages may best be used with assessments made up of convergent questions or questions that have answers within a finite range of accuracy. Weighted scores fall into a different category altogether.

Percentages

Percentages give a good, objective indication of how much of the content was understood. Just make sure that with percentages, 100 percent is the highest a student can achieve, which means he or she understood everything. Anything less than the whole is a smaller percent. If a student goes above-and-beyond assessment expectations, then an extra credit grade may be given. (See the extra credit section that follows for more information.)

Points

The points system also gives a good, objective look at how much a student understands the content. You can have any assessment worth as many points as you want as long as you keep the point "language" intact. In other words, the total value of any one assessment should be on a scale that is compatible to the scale used for others. Points systems work well in fractional form (e.g., the student achieved 150 out of 200 points or 150/200). This evaluation gives a clear picture of how the student fared on the assessment as a whole. For reporting purposes, the score can be translated into a percentage. For the example above, 150/200 = 75%.

Assessments can allow for equal distribution of points for each response. For example, if an assessment has 25 questions or sections, each accurate response would be worth 4 points.

Some assessments may include several sections, some of which are assigned more points than others. For example, an assessment may contain several types of questions, some being convergent and others divergent. In this case, students need to be made aware ahead of time why there is a difference in points earned for these questions. Divergent questions are typically more complex and therefore require a greater depth of knowledge and understanding to answer. Therefore, they are worth more. The responses to the convergent questions may be worth 5 points each, while responses to the divergent questions may be worth 10 points each.

Extra Credit

Extra credit is given when a student goes above and beyond what is required for an assignment. Extra credit can be graded by giving extra percentages or points, which are not added onto or averaged into the assignment grade but rather are listed separately as *Extra Credit*. A student may therefore get 100 percent (or on a point system, 100 out of 100 points) on an assignment and in addition receive 10 percent (or 10 points on a point system) for extra credit work. For example, let's say the assignment has students show the life cycle of a butterfly. Jennifer does so by creating a poster that shows the complete cycle, demonstrating mastery in her understanding of the concepts involved. She receives a score of 100 percent for the assignment. In addition, she also creates another poster showing how the life cycle of a butterfly compares to the life cycle of a plant. The teacher gives her an extra 10 percent (or 10 points based on the grading system being used), entering it under the *Extra Credit* category in the grade book. It is important to note that the two scores must be entered under separate categories. It is also important to note that if the teacher assigns extra credit as an option, the terms for grading must be made clear to students ahead of time.

It is up to the teacher to decide how to report extra-credit work. One option may be to make an anecdotal note on the final report that depicts what extra credit had been completed and what value was assigned to that work. Another option would be to use the extra-credit average scores (per standard) as a means to "bump up" a final grade that is borderline. In any case, students and parents must be aware ahead of time of how extra credit will be used and reported.

Weighted Scores

Weighted scores are a different ball game, and in the name of common sense, I recommend that you do not use them. We are not talking about a separate way of scoring here as with percentages and points. Weighing scores moves into an area that deals with how you are using those points or percentages in relation to content. Weighted scores are defined as "scores in which the components are modified by different multipliers to reflect their relative importance" (Education.com 2012). In other words, components of the assessment are ranked by the teacher by importance and assigned weight accordingly. The focus moves from measuring standards to subjective views of importance.

Let's look at some examples of the use of weighted scores, and then let's look at the logic (or lack of it) of their use in a standards-based system. One example is when a teacher may say, "40 percent of your final grade will be classroom assignments, 40 percent will be test scores, and 20 percent will be homework."

Now let's look at that statement in relation to standards-based assessment and the assessment and evaluation learning curve. Sometimes classroom assignments are formative, and sometimes they are summative. When they are formative, they are considered practice, and those scores do not make it onto the report card. When classroom assignments are summative, the score on the assignment is linked to specific standards and entered in the grade book this way.

Tests are also summative. So they, too, are linked to specific standards, and the scores are entered in the grade book based upon the standards they linked to.

Homework is generally formative, or practice. As formative assessments, therefore, homework scores are not entered into the summative assessment grade book and would not be included in the reporting mix (see Chapter 3). Thus, these scores would not be included in a report card.

So, using the strategy of weighted scores is not appropriate in a standards-based assessment and reporting system. Even with projects, I've heard teachers say, "This project carries more weight on your final grade in this class than any other assignment because it is a culminating activity and is more comprehensive." Let's look at projects with a standards-based perspective. It is true that projects probably cover a lot more content standards than, say, a classroom assignment or a test. So, in a standards-based grade book, there will simply be more standards evaluated and entered into the grade book than there will be for any other summative assignment. Still, we are measuring students against the standard, not one another. Weighted scores simply are not compatible with the practices for reporting that have been discussed here.

Checklists and Rubrics

As Robert Marzano (2000) argues, "Because of the measurement problems associated with average scores, I strongly recommend against their use as a final score for a unit of instruction." Based on this quote, I believe that if Marzano had his way, he might abolish some forms of grading. This would include points and percentages (e.g., grading that is easily and most commonly averaged), and he would possibly turn to a pure society of rubrics! Rubrics are criteria-based, and when you have a list of criteria spelled out for any assessment, students have a better idea of what is expected of them and how they will be judged against the standards.

Checklists

I've heard teachers use the terms *checklist* and *rubric* interchangeably, but they do not mean the same thing. Checklists are planning tools that can be used to create a rubric. A checklist is just what the term implies. It is a list of choices, tasks, or items that must be addressed somehow. The choices, tasks, or items are checked off once they have been completed or the choices have been made. Chapters 3 and 4 discuss examples of checklists. There are checklists for product choices (e.g., *Student Product Menu*). There are checklists for content standards. There are checklists that explicitly state expectations for product quality (e.g., *Quality Criteria*). There are project-planning checklists for task completion. Teachers often create checklists of tasks that they expect students to complete within a given assignment.

Let's revisit the "Characteristics of Mammals" unit. A checklist for accuracy of content on an assessment on this topic might look like the following:

☐ Characteristic 1: has hair or fur

☐ Characteristic 2: live birth

☐ Characteristic 3: breathes oxygen

☐ Characteristic 4: produces milk

☐ Characteristic 5: warm blooded

A checklist for quality of the product might look like the following:

☐ Followed directions

☐ Product is neat

☐ Product is easy to understand

☐ Product is complete

☐ Personal best effort shown

Rubrics

Rubrics, on the other hand, are not so clearly delineated. Rubrics take the items on a content checklist, for example, and break the expectations into detailed levels of quality, accuracy, or completeness. Student-friendly and teacher-friendly rubrics can be easily created from a checklist. Figure 5.1 shows an example of how a content checklist (such as the characteristics of mammals checklist above) can be made into a four-point rubric.

Figure 5.1 Sample Rubric for Accuracy of Content

Characteristic	4	3	2	1	Student Score
hair or fur	Describes *hair or fur* in great detail	Describes *hair or fur* in some detail	Describes *hair or fur* in little or no detail	No description of *hair or fur*	
live birth	Describes *live birth* in great detail	Describes *live birth* in some detail	Describes *live birth* in little or no detail	No description of *live birth*	
breathes oxygen	Describes *breathes oxygen* in great detail	Describes *breathes oxygen* in some detail	Describes *breathes oxygen* in little or no detail	No description of *breathes oxygen*	
produces milk	Describes *produces milk* in great detail	Describes *produces milk* in some detail	Describes *produces milk* in little or no detail	No description of *produces milk*	
warm blooded	Describes *warm blooded* in great detail	Describes *warm blooded* in some detail	Describes *warm blooded* in little or no detail	No description of *warm blooded*	Total Score _____ /20

The score assigned to each characteristic is entered in the last box of each horizontal row. The scores can be added and totaled at the bottom. These individual scores provide a point-based evaluation of how the student performed relative to the assessment task. This total score is appropriate for a standards-based system as it indicates a student's ability to demonstrate understanding of the standard for identifying the characteristics of mammals.

Figure 5.2 shows an example of how the product quality checklist for the same project can be made into a three-point rubric.

Figure 5.2 Rubric for Quality of Product Sample

Category	3	2	1	Student Score
Directions	All directions were followed	Some of the directions were followed	None of the directions were followed	
Neatness	Product meets the highest expectation for neatness	Product meets some expectations for neatness	Product meets very little of the expectations for neatness	
Clarity	Product is easy to understand	Product is somewhat difficult to understand	Product is extremely difficult to understand	
Completeness	Product is complete	Product is somewhat complete	Product is not complete	
Personal Best	Personal best effort is evident	Personal best effort is somewhat evident	Personal best effort is not evident	
			Total Score ___/12	

After a score is entered into each row of this rubric, the scores can be totaled at the bottom as they were for the content rubric. This total provides a points-based evaluation of how the student performed relative to the quality of the product. As a method for evaluating student products, rubrics are very helpful tools. They break down the task of assigning a score to a product by focusing on the important elements and providing concrete criteria to compare the product to.

Please note that the rubric in Figure 5.2 is an example of an assessment of quality and student effort. It does not allow a teacher to evaluate the content of the product in terms of mastery of the targeted standards. In this case, a rubric such as the one exemplified in Figure 5.1 could be created in order for the teacher to accurately evaluate students' mastery of the standards.

What is nice about the use of rubrics, whether they are for content or for quality, is that students get a chance to revise their work using the rubric before turning the assignment in to the teacher. A student should self-assess by using the criteria of the rubric as a guide as he or she is creating the product. Once the product is complete, the student should be given the opportunity to self-evaluate the product. The student will score his or her product using the rubric numbers, thus seeing where revisions and improvements can be made before turning in the final product.

Self-evaluation is simply the act of students judging the quality of their own work. This practice is valuable because it allows for reflection and learning. When a student evaluates his or her own work, he or she is using the proverbial fine-toothed comb to look over and judge every aspect of the assignment before giving it up to the teacher (Bandura 1997). The teacher has the final word on the evaluation of any assessment, but by having students evaluate their own work first, the teacher's job of discerning where and when improvement needs to be made is half done by the time it is turned in!

Recording and Reporting Authentic Assessment Scores

Assessment data must be recorded in a way that will be conducive to how they will be reported. And how they are reported must align with the best practices we are using in the classroom. The following sections will address common-sense strategies for recording and reporting authentic assessment scores, including recording summative scores and reporting the data.

Recording Summative Scores

In Chapter 3, a sample standards-based grade-book page for keeping track of student progress on formative assessments was discussed (see Figure 3.19). The intent is to use this data to drive future instruction. In Chapter 4, the emphasis was placed on giving students ample opportunities to show their new level of mastery. As discussed, a separate grade book should be kept to record summative assessment scores, and this grade book for summative assessments will look quite different. The scores in this grade book page will be transferred onto the final report card.

Let's begin by looking at the possibility of not averaging summative scores for the purpose of coming up with one grade. As an alternative, I would recommend finding the mode. This is the score that most frequently occurs. It is important to note that the mode score sometimes ends up close to the mean score. However, it doesn't always work out that way.

To find the mode, you would first look at the line of summative scores that measure the same standard. For example, Figure 5.3, which identifies percentage scores, may be a typical line on a standards-based, summative grade book page. Figure 5.4 depicts rubric scores.

Figure 5.3 Percentage Scores from a Standards-Based Summative Grade Book

Standard	Summative Assessment Scores							Mode
M5.2—Reads and Interprets Line Graphs	60	78	82	88	89	88	92	88

Figure 5.4 Rubric Scores from a Standards-Based Summative Grade Book

Standard	Summative Assessment Scores							Mode
R3.1—Identifies Main Character	2	3	2	3	3	3	4	3

By taking the mode score, we are apt to have a more valid picture of the student's understanding of the standard. The reason is that by using the mode score, you are taking into account outside circumstances that can affect a student's score on any given assessment. For example, maybe the room was too hot that day, so it affected the student's performance. Or maybe the student's dog died that morning. Maybe he or she just got lucky and made some good guesses on some of the answers. Perhaps the type of assessment was not the best way for the student to show understanding of the content (e.g., it was a written test and he or she is not a strong writer, which affects his or her ability to show content knowledge).

Let's see how finding the mean score instead of the mode would affect the list of scores shown above. If the scores in Figure 5.3 were averaged rather than finding the mode, the student would have achieved only an 82 rather than an 88 on this standard.

The scores in both Figure 5.3 and Figure 5.4 show how the student is progressing over time as that student climbs the learning curve through practice and eventually, mastery. Accuracy is compromised when practice scores or margins of error are averaged into final summative scores. Keep in mind that mode focuses on patterns, not on isolated scores. Finding mode scores works to show a truer picture of students' standing at report card time.

Robert Marzano (2000) supports this notion of mode vs. mean in grading. Along those lines, as I've said before, short, frequent assessments are more effective than long, infrequent ones. If you have provided students with frequent opportunities to show mastery of a standard via summative assessment, you should have a good range of scores from which to calculate the mode.

Scores in the summative grade book make it onto the report card, whereas formative scores do not. Therefore, the types of scores you use must be compatible with the grading format of your school's report card. Does the report card ask for percentages? Points? Rubrics? Letter grades? Whatever the report card asks for, use that same grade type in your summative grade book for easy transition onto the report card. This may require some conversions on individual assessments (e.g., rubrics or points converted to percentages).

Figures 5.5 and 5.6 are samples of grade book pages for summative assessments. These encompass my recommendation for a valid view of student progress toward mastery of standards. Figure 5.5 uses mode for percentages to arrive at one score per standard. Please note that only one row of Quality scores is recorded as this is simply for example purposes.

Figure 5.5 Summative Grade Book Using Mode for Percentage Scores

Content Area: Math Quarter 1

Standard/Activity	M1.2—Prob & Stats	M1.2—Graphs Galore	M1.2—Chapter Test	M1.2—Problem Solver	M1.2—Data Project	MODE Score	M1.4—Angle Answers	M1.4—Ray Recollections	M1.4—Shapes Project	M1.4—3-D Replica	M1.4—Unit Test	MODE Score	Avg. Mode*
Students/Quality													
Blevins, Jeremy	85	95	88	95	95	(95)	80	95	90	94	100	(93)	(94)
Quality	81	78	80	82	94	(81)	80	80	100	80	60	(80)	(81)
Brown, Betsy	88	90	90	92	90	(90)	69	79	95	87	100	(94)	(92)
Quality													
Carpenter, Mindy	85	79	85	93	85	(85)	78	79	92	90	87	(91)	(88)
Quality													
Dempsey, Paul	85	90	85	95	95	(95)	82	90	95	94	100	(93)	(94)
Quality													

*Use only when one score must be entered on a content-based report card

Sometimes there will be no mode for a set of scores. If a student's set of scores does not have a mode, consider these other ways to calculate a score for that standard:

- Find a range in which the majority of student's scores fall (e.g., 70s, 80s, 90s). Average all of the scores that fall into this range. For example, if the majority of scores fall in the 80s, find the average of those scores (e.g., the average of 85, 83, 86, 80 is 84%).

- If all scores fall into completely different number ranges, average the scores that fall in the top three number ranges. In Figure 5.5, Betsy Brown's scores for standard M1.4 show this. Her scores are 69, 79, 95, 87, and 100. In this case, you would take the top three scores (87, 95, and 100) and average them, resulting in a final score of 94. In keeping with the idea of using the mode, remember that any time the majority of scores falls into higher number ranges, chances are that the student understands that standard at that level of proficiency.

- If two or more sets of scores fall within the same number range (e.g., two scores in the 70s, two scores in the 80s, two scores in the 90s), average the scores that fall into the highest number range. In Figure 5.5, Mindy Carpenter's scores for standard M1.4 show an example of this. Mindy received two scores that fell within the 90s range (90 and 92), and two scores that fell within the 70s range (79 and 78). So, you would take the average of the scores in the higher range (90s) to find a score of 91. Again, remember that any time the majority of scores falls into higher number ranges, chances are that the student understands the standard at that level of proficiency.

Figure 5.6 uses mode for rubrics to arrive at one score per standard. Please note that only one row of Quality scores is recorded as this is simply for example purposes. Also, note that some of the same techniques for finding a final score per standard when no mode is present can be used for this as well. For example, if there's no mode, average students' top few scores. Paul Dempsey's M1.4 mode score is an example of this. His set of scores were all unique (e.g., 3, 2, 5, 4, 6), so the highest three numbers (4, 5, and 6) were averaged together to find a mean score of 5. Or if a student has frequently recurring numbers, such as Mindy Carpenter's set of scores for M1.2 in which there are equal numbers of 3s and 4s, use the higher number for the final mode score.

Figure 5.6 Summative Grade Book Using Mode for Rubric Scores

Content Area: Math Quarter 1

Standard/Activity	M1.2—Prob & Stats	M1.2—Graphs Galore	M1.2—Chapter Tes	M1.2—Problem Solver	M1.2—Data Project	MODE Score	M1.4—Angle Answers	M1.4—Ray Recollections	M1.4—Shapes Project	M1.4—3-D Replica	M1.4—Unit Test	MODE Score	Avg. Mode*
Students													
Blevins, Jeremy	5	5	4	3	5	⑤	6	5	6	4	6	⑥	⑥
Quality	1	2	2	2	3	②	2	3	3	3	2	③	③
Brown, Betsy	3	3	4	5	3	③	3	2	4	4	5	④	④
Quality													
Carpenter, Mindy	4	3	3	5	4	④	6	2	5	5	5	⑤	⑤
Quality													
Dempsey, Paul	3	4	4	2	3	④	3	2	5	4	6	⑤	⑤
Quality													

*Use only when one score must be entered on a content-based report card

A blank template of a summative grade book that factors in mode scores is found in Appendix A. You can use it as an exercise to see how your students' evaluations would look in this type of system.

If, for some reason, you must whittle down the mode or mean scores even further into one final score for the content area, then the mode or mean scores for each standard can be averaged. This is depicted in the last column on Figures 5.5 and 5.6. I do not recommend doing this, however, as the data becomes diluted and the emphasis on measuring students against the standards is lost. I understand, however, that you may find yourself under reporting restrictions that you cannot control, so I wanted to be sure to represent how this can be done, if necessary.

Reporting the Data

Now you have seen how to enter summative assessment scores into a standards-based grade book. We know that these are the only scores that should be reported on a final report card. Some grade books (online or otherwise) may also serve as a reporting tool. They are a grade book and report card all rolled into one. Whatever form the report card takes, make certain you are doing what you can to use a tool that allows for valid reporting of data (e.g., summative assessments) and alignment with state or national standards.

Does your reporting tool handle various types of evaluation (e.g., rubrics, points, and percentages)? In a perfect world, the ideal reporting tool would automatically convert the various types of evaluation into one. For example, any rubric scores, points, and percentages imported from the summative grade book onto the reporting tool would be automatically converted into percentages for the sake of continuity on the report card. Your reporting system may do this, and if so, you are a step ahead of many!

Unfortunately, many existing reporting tools do not accept varying forms of evaluation. The danger, then, is that teachers may take the path of least resistance and score everything using one type of evaluation format just so that it will be easy to enter into the reporting tool. Ask yourself this: Are you choosing appropriate evaluation formats to fit the assessments or do you select them to fit the reporting tool? Hopefully it is the former, not the latter.

Let me give you some ideas for how you can make those conversions in order to keep true scores taken from the various evaluation forms you entered into your grade book and still accommodate your current reporting tool. This conversion process is not what many researchers would condone. But since many of us do not have that perfect-world reporting tool, I will show you how you can still use various forms of evaluations for your assessments and be able to enter them onto a reporting tool that will only accept one form—in this case, percentages.

This will require some calculations on your part after you have entered the scores in your grade book. Once the calculations are done, you would enter the converted score onto the reporting tool. Many of you may already do this on your own and have devised your own system for making these conversions. I will err on the safe side by including a sample conversion chart that I have used when it was necessary to make those conversions (see Figure 5.7). Hopefully, this will help you use the true scores you entered throughout the grading period in your grade books rather than revert to scoring every assessment with percentages simply because that's all your report card will accept.

Figure 5.7 Converting True Assessment Scores to Fit Traditional Reporting Systems

Rubrics to Percents		Percents to Letter Grades	
True Score	Percent	True Score	Letter Grade
5	100%	100%	A+
4	80%	90%	A
3	60%	80%	B
2	40%	70%	C
1	20%	60%	D
0	No Data	50%	F

Of course, rubrics can have many levels to them. To convert these levels to percentages, simply divide the total number of points earned on the rubric by the total number of points possible. For example, the conversion of 10 points earned on a rubric totaling 12 points would look like this: 10/12 = 83%. Eight points earned, for example, on that same rubric would look like this: 8/12 = 67%.

Report Cards Versus Progress Reports

Common sense and current pedagogies suggest that reporting tools should reflect the way teachers teach. So let's look at report cards and progress reports. What we call our reporting tools may seem insignificant, but the differences in what their names infer are huge. The language of these labels sets the stage for how teachers use them.

Report Cards

This name suggests a card that simply reports. Reports what? It could report anything, but traditionally they report grades and possibly behavior, though some report cards do not allow space for this. Because of the way they are entered and presented, grades and behavior marks are one size fits all. They show one state of learning in one subject area at one point in time (e.g., English, B, fourth quarter). What do those marks represent?

I admit that I have been guilty of buying into that frozen moment and judging my own children harshly on that basis. "What? You got a C in math this quarter? How did that happen? Last quarter you got a B! You need to study harder. As a matter of fact, if you raise your grade next quarter, I'll give you five dollars!" Well, I didn't really pay my kids for their grades, but you get the picture.

I am an educator and have been for many years. I know better than to buy into that now. Yet at first glance of that notorious report card, my initial reaction is horror or elation, depending on the marks that glare out from the white pages of "the card." And why shouldn't they glare? The emphasis of the report card is not on what the marks mean or what they are measuring. The emphasis is on the marks themselves because that's all the information that is given to us besides a reference to subject area. And even though we now know better, there still may be limitations to what you as a teacher can do.

What if your school report card does not allow you to report only summative assessments? You may be surprised at how many reporting systems actually have a means by which you can delete scores from final grade averages. More intensive training on the tool itself may be needed to realize what the system can actually do.

What if your school report card is not standards-based? This is not unusual, even in the standards-driven world of education we live in today. I still see report cards that replicate the report cards of the '50s, which list the content areas and boast letter grades. Those outdated report cards look something like this: Math: A, Reading: B+, Social Studies: C… you get the picture. Every public school in every state in the United States is mandated to teach the standards, and the students are assessed yearly on these standards. Yet so many schools are still using report cards that are not aligned to those standards. What is the result? The bottom line is that what students do in the classroom must be reported, so teachers fashion their assessments and lesson plans to fit the format of the report card. When the report card categorizes grades by content area, the teacher ends up teaching textbook chapters rather than standards. The table of contents becomes the scope and sequence, not the standards. It is the path of least resistance. It is what the report card asks for.

When I work with teachers and administrators on the topic of assessment and reporting, I ask them, "Are you teaching to your report card? Or are you modifying your report card to reflect the way you teach?" What should it be? The latter. Your job now as a teacher and an educator is to study how you evaluate and record student assessments. Then, take a look at how you report this data. Are you using research-based best practices in these areas, which include the examples I have given you in this section? Are you using your common sense? If there are changes that need to be made, plan on making them. You can start by taking the baby steps I suggested for modifying the reporting tool to reflect the way you assess your students. Volunteer to be on the next report card committee. Your input as a teacher "working in the trenches" is valuable, especially when there are changes to be made.

Progress Reports

The name says it all. Not only does the name say that we will see progress, but it is also telling us this is a report of that progress. When I think of the word *progress*, what immediately comes to mind is a continuum. The student has just spent time climbing a learning curve through pre-assessment, formative assessment, and finally summative assessment. He or she has made the journey to reach the goal of mastery. That is what a continuum shows. Does your reporting tool show continuous progress toward a goal? When we can see the big picture, and a continuum will do that for us, we are given the past, the present, and a hopeful future all in one glance, similar to a time line.

Even a standards-based reporting tool can fall into either category of *report card* or *progress report*. Granted, standards-based report cards as opposed to subject-based report cards at least give more information on exactly what was studied and measured within the subject area. With such a format, I am able to see that yes, my child got a 78 percent in these certain mathematics standards this quarter as compared to the 95 percent last quarter, and the progress report format I will introduce also gives some clues as to why that may have happened. When the standards are specifically laid out, it is clear that the content, as depicted by the standards, changed from the first quarter to the next. The content may be more complex than last quarter, and that's why he received that lower mark. You would hope that parents (and the students themselves, for that matter) would already know that a student's grade may lower because the content changes. But don't assume that they know this.

One score on the report card, even next to a standard, still does not show how the student has progressed from one quarter or one subsection of the grading period to the next. The ideal progress report divides the content areas into specific standards and also shows the student's progress toward mastery of those standards. This is the common-sense approach to reporting. It absolutely aligns with how we should be teaching in our classrooms. It shows continuous progress depicting a starting point and then progress toward mastery.

Figure 5.8 is an abbreviated and simplified example of a standards-based continuous progress report. Study its components and use it as food for thought for possible implementation of a new progress reporting system. Each standard is identified as well as the grading period (in this case, the quarter).

Let's say this is a section of Leon's report card for language arts. For standard 1LA, he achieved 50 percent toward mastery by the end of the first quarter, which is depicted by the bar on the graph next to *Standard 1LA* and the *Q1* label. He continued working on this same language arts standard and achieved 98 percent toward mastery by the end of the second quarter. Language arts standard 3LA was not covered in the first quarter, as evident by the absence of a bar labeled *Q1*. Leon achieved 60 percent mastery of that standard by the end of the second quarter. For standard 4LA, Leon achieved 90 percent mastery by the end of quarter one and continued on to a level of 95 percent in the second quarter. All of these summative mode scores were calculated from the summative grade book and transferred onto this graph.

Figure 5.8 Standards-Based Progress Report Sample

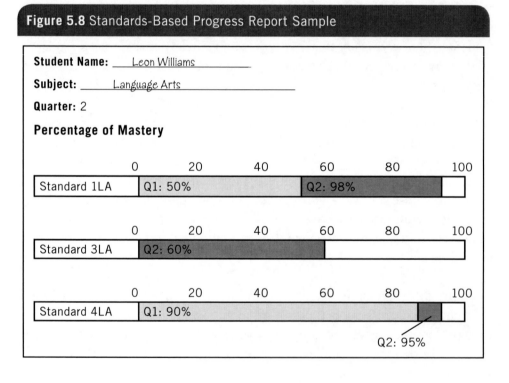

This sample may seem out of reach to you because of valid concerns, such as district restraints, lack of time to research options, and restrictive online reporting tools. I understand these concerns, and they are all real. But do take some steps in the direction of standards-based reporting that shows continuous progress. You can start by doing some or all of these suggestions:

- Spend time reflecting on and discussing with your colleagues ways in which you can make the reporting tool you now use compatible with how you are currently teaching, assessing, and evaluating students according to the standards-based curriculum.

- Brainstorm and list ideas that will help you achieve the goal of standards-based reporting and submit them to your administrators.

- Form a report card committee and delegate tasks. Research continuous progress reporting tools that are already being used by school districts. Find out what is working and what is not by going online and searching through information from schools that are using these tools.

- Strive to emulate the standards-based continuous progress reporting as closely as possible.

You've gotten this far in the book, so you have already taken a big step in your journey to a common-sense approach to assessment and grading in your school. The next and final chapter will give you a step-by-step guide for how to proceed from this point on.

Review and Reflect

1. Students are adept at comparing themselves to other students when it comes to achievement. What have you done or what can you do to focus their attention on their progress against the standards and not on their progress in relation to other students?

2. In this chapter, I posed the question *Are we teaching to fit our reporting tool or are we modifying our reporting tool to fit the way we teach?* What does this mean to you? How feasible is it for you to modify the way you report student progress? What can you do to improve your reporting tool?

3. Reflect on how weighted scores are not consistent with a standards-based grading system. How can you make adjustments to this practice in your classroom?

4. What do you think are the benefits of using mode scores in reporting? What may be some pitfalls?

6

Where Do I Start?

"Measurements are not to provide numbers but insight."

—Ingrid Bucher (1987)

Assessment and Grading Self-Evaluation

It is imperative to pre-assess students before starting a unit to see where they are and where they need to go. For the same reasons, it is also a good idea for you to do so with your professional practices related to assessment and grading before you set up a plan for change. Find out where you are so that you can concentrate on areas where you need to move forward.

Once you have pre-assessed where you are with your assessment and grading practices, develop an action plan that will be your road map for becoming an assessment master! You will *practice, practice, practice* just like your students. Every so often, survey yourself again to see what you have achieved, where you still need to improve, and what you may need to revise your action plan.

Figure 6.1, *Assessment and Grading Self-Evaluation*, is a survey that teachers and administrators alike can use. Check the appropriate box after each statement. Or you can develop your own based on the criteria for common sense assessment mentioned throughout this book. Whatever you use, consider it your "curriculum map" for achieving your highest goals for mastery of the content for assessment best practices. This resource can be found in Appendix A.

When you have completed the survey, pat yourself on the back for all of the boxes you checked in the *Always* column. The boxes you checked in the *Sometimes* column are areas you can address later in the year. The boxes you checked in the *Never* column are where you want to start. Prioritize them, and then work to change them one at a time as you feel comfortable.

Practical First Steps

You may be feeling a little overwhelmed after reading this book. I have presented many strategies and ideas for common sense assessment and grading.

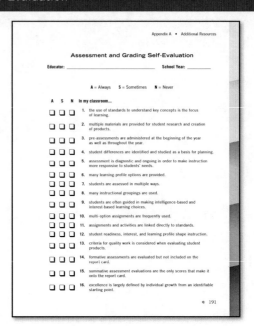

Figure 6.1 Assessment and Grading Self-Evaluation

Even more overwhelming and perhaps perplexing may be the notion that you may have to change your thinking first before you can make changes in your district, school, or classroom.

Through the years, traditional ways of assessing and grading have become ingrained in our thought processes and have been manifested into the systems we've created in our educational environments. Tradition is powerful because the way we have "always done it" is the only model we have. Thus, tradition is perpetuated.

Change takes time. Shifting your way of thinking about assessment and grading is going to take time. Going from traditional thinking to new thinking in any field is a process. Take this process one step at a time. What follows is a broad step-by-step guide for creating a common sense assessment and grading system in your standards-based classroom or school.

Start with the first step, do it, and when it's complete, go to the next. Don't try to cram too many tasks in at once. The danger is that if you start to feel overwhelmed, you may chuck it all and decide to take the path of least resistance and stop doing it altogether. Make this list into a checklist to remind yourself to take the steps one at a time.

Step #1: Start with your standards.

Make sure you know and understand which standards you are supposed to teach for mastery at your grade level. Make a simple list from the Common Core State Standards and/or your state's standards. Include only those standards that are targeted for mastery. Do this for every content area or grade level that you teach. You cannot begin to teach until you know what standards you are assessing and measuring.

Step #2: Post the Assessment and Evaluation Learning Curve.

Post the learning curve on a wall in your classroom and start the climb with your students. For every unit, post the standards that will be addressed in that unit. Students need to see them, and you do, too, as a daily reminder that you are teaching standards and not chapters of textbooks. Then, pre-assess your students' learning profiles, interests, and readiness for content. Do this to address the diverse learners in your differentiated classroom.

Step #3: For every lesson, every day, assess, assess, assess!

Differentiate assessments to meet the needs of your students. In your lesson plans, label the assignments and activities as *formative*, and eventually, when students have had ample time to practice in their own time and in their own way, label them as *summative*. Labeling the assessments in your plans is a great way to remind yourself to keep your eye on the learning curve!

Step #4: Modify your reporting tool to reflect the way you teach.

Sign up to be on the report card committee in your school to search for the perfect tool that is standards-based, allows for differentiated assessments, has the capability of calculating only summative assessments for final reporting, and shows student progress over time.

Step #5: Be vigilant and attend workshops.

Be vigilant in staying current on assessment and grading research and differentiated instruction pedagogy. Attend workshops. Read education journals. And most importantly, integrate these strategies into your classroom practices, one baby step at a time.

Review and Reflect

1. What steps will you take right now to implement common sense assessment and grading in your classroom?

2. How can you create mentorships in your learning community to support you as you try new ways of assessing and grading in your classroom?

Name: _____ Date: _____

How Are You Smart?

blue	yellow	red	green	orange	purple	black	pink

blue = logical/mathematical
yellow = verbal/linguistic

red = visual/spatial
green = musical/rhythmical

orange = bodily/kinesthetic
purple = naturalist/environmental

black = interpersonal
pink = intrapersonal

Multiple Intelligences Behavior Inventory Grades K–2

Directions: Use with *How Are You Smart?* Tell students to color in one square with the appropriate color if the sentence describes them.

Logical/Mathematical

I like to work with calculators and computers.
I like to work with numbers.
I can count or add quickly in my head.
I like to play math games.

Bodily/Kinesthetic

Riding bikes or skating is easy for me.
When I speak, I use my hands and move my body.
I am good at building things with my hands.
I enjoy dancing, jumping rope, or moving around the room.

Verbal/Linguistic

I like to listen to people talk.
I can use big words when I talk.
I like to write stories.
I like to read.

Naturalist/Environmental

I keep collections of things.
I know about bugs and animals and how to tell them apart.
I like to see how things feel when I touch them.
I like to take long walks outside, mostly to smell the outdoors, enjoy the weather, and watch for animals and insects.

Visual/Spatial

I do not get lost easily.
I enjoy putting puzzles together.
I would rather draw pictures than write sentences.
I can tell how far away something is without measuring, and I can tell how many objects are in a jar without counting them.

Interpersonal

I enjoy being with groups of other children.
I can tell when my friends are happy or sad.
I have lots of friends.
I like being part of a team.

Musical/Rhythmical

I enjoy playing a musical instrument.
One of my favorite things to do is listen to music.
I like to hum, whistle, or sing.
Music can make me happy, and it can make me sad.

Intrapersonal

I enjoy quiet time alone.
I remember my dreams.
When I go places with my family, I like to save things that I have found there.
I am comfortable playing by myself.

Name: _____ Date: _____

Which Intelligence Are You?

10								
9								
8								
7								
6								
5								
4								
3								
2								
1								
	logical/ mathematical	verbal/ linguistic	visual/ spatial	musical/ rhythmical	bodily/ kinesthetic	naturalist/ environmental	interpersonal	intrapersonal

What does this graph say about how you learn?

_____

_____

_____

Multiple Intelligences Behavior Inventory Grades 3–8

Directions: Read each statement below. Tell students to mark a 1 if the statement does not describe them at all, a 10 if the statement describes them perfectly, or a number in between if the statement sort of describes them.

Logical/Mathematical

I can add or multiply quickly in my head. I like to work with calculators. I like to play number and strategy games. I can see patterns and relationships between numbers quickly and easily. I like to work with numbers and figures.

Bodily/Kinesthetic

I pick up new dance steps quickly. Learning to ride a bike or skate was easy. My sense of balance and coordination is good. I enjoy building models or sculpting. I'm good at athletics.

Verbal/Linguistic

It is easy for me to say what I think in an argument or debate. I enjoy a good lecture, speech, or debate. I am irritated when I hear an argument or statement that sounds illogical. I enjoy reading and building my vocabulary. I'm good at finding the fine points of word meanings. I'd like to study the structure and logic of languages.

Naturalist/Environmental

I feel at home outdoors and in natural surroundings. Taking care of the environment is a high priority. I love to explore and to experiment. Factual science and social studies information gives me quality enjoyment time. I relate well to animals and enjoy the responsibility of caring for them. I am sensitive to the sights, sounds, and feel of things around me.

Visual/Spatial

I would rather draw a map than give someone verbal directions. I always know North from South no matter where I am. I always understand the directions that come with new gadgets or appliances. I can look at an object one way and see it turned sideways or backwards just as easily.

Interpersonal

I'm sensitive to the expressions on other's faces. I am sensitive to the moods of others. I have a good sense of what other people think of me. I like working in a group.

Musical/Rhythmical

I can play or used to play a musical instrument. I can associate music with my moods. Life seems empty without music. I often connect a piece of music with some event in my life. I like to hum, whistle, and sing even when I'm alone.

Intrapersonal

People say they can read my face like a book. I stay "in touch" with my moods. I have no trouble identifying what I'm feeling. I prefer to work alone.

Multiple Intelligences Behavior Inventory Grades 9–12

Directions: Read each statement below. Tell students to mark a 1 if the statement does not describe them at all, a 10 if the statement describes them perfectly, or a number in between if the statement sort of describes them.

Logical/Mathematical

I am good at finding and understanding patterns. I am quick at solving a variety of problems mentally. I can remember formulas and strategies. I like to identify and sort things into categories. I am able to follow complex lines of reasoning and thought processes.

Verbal/Linguistic

I love talking, writing, and reading almost anything. I precisely express myself in writing and speaking. I enjoy public speaking. I am sensitive to the impact of words and language on others. I understand and enjoy plays on words and word games.

Visual/Spatial

I frequently doodle during class activities. I am helped by visuals and manipulatives. I like painting, drawing, and working with my hands. I have a good sense of direction and understanding of maps. I create mental images easily. I like to daydream.

Musical/Rhythmical

I hum quietly to myself while working or walking. I tap my pencil, foot, or fingers while working. I can remember songs and rhymes easily. I like to make up tunes and melodies. I sense musical elements in unusual or nonmusical situations.

Bodily/Kinesthetic

I have difficulty sitting still or staying in my seat. I use body gestures and physical movement to express myself. I am good at sports. I am well-coordinated physically. I like to invent things, put things together, and take them apart. I like to demonstrate to others how to do something.

Naturalist/Environmental

I am drawn to the natural environment. I am sensitive to the sights, sounds, smells, and feelings of things around me. I am curious about and interested in animals and insects. I want to grow things. I love plants and flowers. I frequently comment on things that happen in the natural world.

Interpersonal

I have an irresistible urge to discuss almost everything with others. I am good at listening and communicating. I sense the moods and feelings of others. I am a good, effective team player. I am able to figure out the motives and intentions of others.

Intrapersonal

I am highly intuitive and adaptable. I am quiet, very self-reflective, introspective, and aware. I ask questions relentlessly. I have an avid curiosity. I am able to express inner feelings in a variety of ways. I am individualistic and independent. I am not concerned about others' opinions.

Multiple Intelligences Observation Checklist: Tally Student Behaviors

Intelligence ▲ Student ▶	Logical/ Mathematical Likes to experiment with and explore numbers and patterns	Verbal/ Linguistic Likes to play with words in reading, writing, and speaking	Visual/Spatial Likes to put visualizations into drawing, building, designing, and creating	Musical/ Rhythmical Sings, hums, plays instruments; generally responds and learns to music	Bodily/ Kinesthetic Likes to dance, play sports, do crafts; learns through movement and touch	Naturalist/ Environmental Likes to explore, experiment; be outdoors; sensitive to sights, sounds, feel of things around them	Interpersonal Shares, cooperates, has lots of friends; learns with and from others	Intrapersonal Likes to work along at own pace, producing original, unique work

About Me!

Directions: Complete each sentence with information about yourself.

My name is: _____

I love to: _____

_____

My favorite thing to do is: _____

_____

My favorite subject in school is: _____

_____

My favorite book is: _____

_____

I am really good at: _____

_____

I am not that good at: _____

_____

My favorite person is: _____

_____

I like this person because: _____

_____

About Me!

Directions: Complete each sentence with information about yourself.

My name is: _____

I love: _____

_____

In my free time, I usually: _____

_____

My favorite activities are: _____

_____

I like the following types of math problems: _____

_____

I read books, such as these, on my own time: _____

_____

My favorite activities on the computer are: _____

_____

I have the following special abilities and talents: _____

_____

Special concerns I have are: _____

_____

My most notable moments during the past year are: _____

_____

_____

The person I look up to the most is: _____

_____

I look up to this person because: _____

_____

About My Child

Child's Name: _____

Directions: Circle the appropriate letter for each statement. Do not circle anything for statements that do not apply.

A = Always **S** = Sometimes **N** = Never

My child...

A **S** **N** is very aware of physical surroundings.

A **S** **N** asks questions about ideas like love, feelings, relationships, or justice.

A **S** **N** needs less sleep than other children of the same age.

A **S** **N** moves around a lot; is very physically active.

A **S** **N** talked early.

A **S** **N** has a long attention span for activities that interest him or her.

A **S** **N** is extremely concerned and curious about the meaning of life and death.

A **S** **N** reacts strongly to noise, light, taste, smell, or touch.

A **S** **N** craves stimulation and activity; rarely content to sit idle.

A **S** **N** can be emotional and cries, angers, and excites easily.

A **S** **N** has an excellent memory.

A **S** **N** insists that people be fair; complains when things are unfair.

A **S** **N** is extremely curious and asks *Why? How? What if...?*

A **S** **N** becomes so involved that he or she is "lost in his or her own world."

A **S** **N** explains ideas in complex, unusual ways.

A **S** **N** is very interested in cause-effect relationships.

A **S** **N** reasons well; thinks of creative ways to solve problems.

A **S** **N** is very interested in calendars, clocks, maps, and structures.

A **S** **N** has a vivid imagination; may have trouble separating real from unreal.

A **S** **N** is extremely creative; uses materials in unusual ways.

About My Child *(cont.)*

A   S   N   sees many possible answers and solutions.

A   S   N   spends free time drawing, painting, writing, or sculpting.

A   S   N   has a spontaneous and/or advanced sense of humor.

A   S   N   likes to play with words; uses advanced vocabulary.

A   S   N   often sings or moves rhythmically; may communicate by singing.

A   S   N   memorizes tunes and lyrics.

A   S   N   often prefers playing with older children or being with adults.

A   S   N   creates and plays complicated games.

A   S   N   gives complex answers to questions.

A   S   N   becomes frustrated when his or her body can't do what his or her mind wants it to.

A   S   N   has a strong sense of self-control and wants to know reasons for rules.

A   S   N   is eager to try new things.

A   S   N   can concentrate on two or three activities at one time.

Parent/Caregiver's Signature: _____   **Date:** _____

Ticket In Pre-Assessment

Name: _____ **Date:** _____

Directions: Complete the chart with information you know about the topic.

What do you know about the topic?	**What words can you use to describe the topic?**

Topic

Is this topic interesting to you? Why or why not?	**What do you want to know about this topic?**

Anticipation Guide

Name: _____   **Date:** _____

Topic: Christopher Columbus

Directions: Mark each answer *T* for true or *F* for false.

_____ Christopher Columbus was determined to prove Earth was flat.

_____ Christopher Columbus asked Queen Isabella of Spain for ships and sailors to discover the way to the Philippines.

_____ When Christopher Columbus landed after weeks of sailing the ocean, he thought that he was in the Indies. He named the people who lived there *Indians*.

_____ Christopher Columbus sailed to many other islands.

_____ Christopher Columbus spent time in jail in Spain, but soon Queen Isabella freed him.

Concept Mind Map

Name: _____ **Date:** _____

Directions: Complete the chart with information you know about the concept.

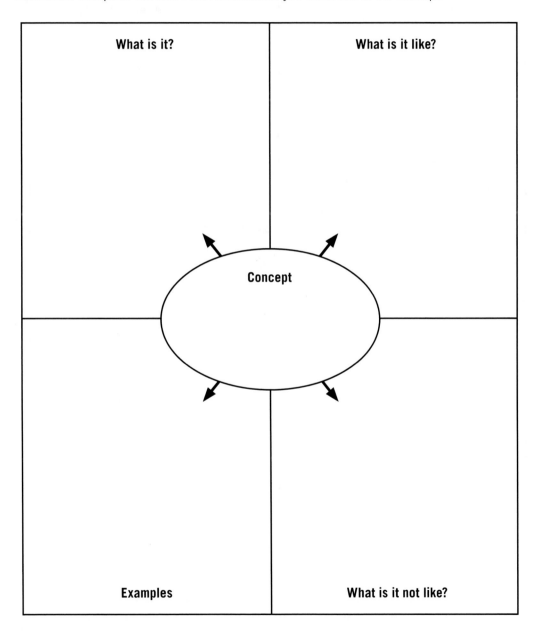

Prescription for Differentiation

Name: _____   **Date:** _____

Learning Styles	Multiple Intelligences

Prescription

Interests	Readiness for Content

Student Product Menu 1

Name: _____

Content/Standard: _____

_____

_____

Directions: Check the box that tells how you will show the information you know.

❑ **Draw a picture.**

❑ **Act it out.**

❑ **Write a letter.**

❑ **Write a song and sing it.**

❑ **Tell the teacher.**

My idea:_____

_____

_____

_____

Student Product Menu 2

Name: _____

Content/Standard: _____

_____

_____

Directions: Check the box that tells you how you will show the information you know.

☐ comic strip	☐ pamphlet
☐ detailed illustration	☐ poetry
☐ diary entry	☐ short essay
☐ flip book	☐ song
☐ graph	☐ radio program
☐ illustrated story	☐ time line
☐ letter	☐ voice recording
☐ painting	☐ other

My idea: _____

_____

_____

Student Product Menu 3

Name: _____

Content/Standard: _____

_____

_____

Directions: Check the box that tells you how you will show the information you know.

☐ 3-D model   ☐ skit

☐ diagram   ☐ song

☐ letter   ☐ story

☐ picture   ☐ voice recording

☐ poem   ☐ other

My idea: _____

_____

_____

_____

_____

_____

_____

_____

Research Menu

Name: _____

Content/Standard: _____

_____

_____

Directions: Check the box that tells you how you will conduct your research.

❑ handout

❑ Internet

❑ interview a student

❑ interview a teacher

❑ posted classroom visuals

❑ textbook

Other: _____

_____

_____

_____

Activity Response Sheet 1

Name: _____ **Date:** _____

Activity: _____

_____

Directions: Write your answers below.

_____

_____

_____

_____

_____

_____

_____

Activity Response Sheet 2

Name: _____ **Date:** _____

Activity: _____

_____

Directions: Write your response on the lines below.

_____

_____

_____

_____

_____

_____

_____

_____

_____

_____

_____

_____

_____

_____

_____

_____

_____

_____

_____-Tac-Toe

Name: _____ **Date:** _____

Directions: Complete three activities in one horizontal row, one vertical row, or on the major diagonal line.

Standards targeted: _____

_____

_____

Math-Tac-Toe

Name: _____ **Date:** _____

Directions: Complete three activities in one horizontal row, one vertical row, or on the major diagonal line.

Make a pie graph that shows how you spend your allowance money. Tell why you spend your allowance the way you do.	Cut out a picture from a magazine. Then, create a graph using information from your picture. For example, use career types, brands of shoes, or plant categories. Be creative!	Cut out a graph from a newspaper or magazine. Write five questions that the graph could answer.
Make a chart showing the kinds and amounts of food you eat in one day, including how many total calories you consume. Comment on foods you like and foods you dislike but eat anyway.	How many letters are in your first and last name? Which letters: • appear most frequently? • appear only once? • are vowels? • are consonants? Make a chart of all this information.	Make a survey of the number of phones, bathrooms, bedrooms, chairs, windows, and clocks in your home. Present the results in a chart.
Looking at a small bag of multicolored candies, guess how many of each color are in the bag. Show your guesses and then the actual counts on a bar graph, pictograph, or line graph.	Design a product and create an ad to promote its sale. Explain why your product is worth the price you are charging. Include a bar graph or chart that will support your explanation.	Name five occupations. Then, list them in order of the salary you think they deserve, from highest to lowest. Put this information in a chart or graph. Tell why you ranked each career the way you did.

Standard(s) targeted: Understands and interprets charts and graphs

Reading-Tac-Toe

Name: _____ **Date:** _____

Directions: Complete three activities in one horizontal row, one vertical row, or on the major diagonal line.

What are the main character's strengths and weaknesses? Include evidence from the story.	Compare and contrast the personality of the main character with those of other characters in the story. Include evidence from the story.	Show how the personality of the main character changed over time in the story. Include evidence from the story.
Do you agree or disagree with the main character's actions and/or behaviors? Why?	How is the main character the same as you? How is he or she different from you? Include examples from the story and your life.	Could the main character be your best friend? Why or why not?
Predict how the end of the story might have been affected if the main character had made a different decision along the way.	Associate the main character with a celebrity. What traits do they both share? Give specific examples.	You are the main character, and the book is your autobiography. How would you persuade the public to read your book?

Standard(s) targeted: Understands elements of character development in literary works

Quality Criteria

Name: _____ **Date:** _____

Directions: Check the boxes that describe your work.

☐ Did you follow directions?

☐ Is it neat?

☐ Is it easy to understand?

☐ Is it complete?

☐ Is it your personal best?

☐ Other: _____

Other Possible Criteria

Is your work original? (i.e., Is it yours, or did you get it from the Internet, your parents, or a peer?)

Does it make sense?

Is the targeted standard addressed?

Standards-Based Scoring of Formative/ Summative Assessments

Name: _____   **Date:** _____

Content/Standards: _____

_____

Key Content (Based on the Standard)	Evaluation
1.	
2.	
3.	
4.	
5.	
Final Evaluation (Content/Standard)	

Quality Criteria	Evaluation
1.	
2.	
3.	
4.	
5.	
Final Evaluation (Quality)	

Ticket Out

Name: _____ **Date:** _____

Directions: Answer each question below.

What did you learn about the topic?	**Is this topic interesting to you? Why or why not?**
What words or pictures can you use to describe the topic?	**What else do you want to know about this topic?**

Exit Cards

Name: _____ **Date:** _____

Directions: Answer each question below.

What confirmed something you already knew about the topic?

What did you see from a new angle?

What question is going around in your mind?

Making Faces

Name: _____   **Date:** _____

Activity: _____

Directions: Read the question. If the answer is yes, draw a smile on the *Yes* face. If the answer is no, draw a frown on the *No* face.

Did I share my ideas?

Did I help with the product?

Did I finish on time?

Prescriptive Differentiation Planning Chart

Standard/Concept: _____

_____

Pre-Assessments: _____

_____

Readiness Levels (List student names)	Concepts/Skills Known	Prescription
Still Don't Get It!		
Getting There!		
Got It!		

Intelligences Project Planning Menu

Name: _____

Unit of Study: _____

Date: _____ **Goal Date for Completion:** _____

Standards/Content: _____

_____

❑ **Logical/Mathematical Product:** _____

Content: _____

❑ **Verbal/Linguistic Product:** _____

Content: _____

❑ **Visual/Spatial Product:** _____

Content: _____

❑ **Musical/Rhythmical Product:** _____

Content: _____

❑ **Bodily/Kinesthetic Product:** _____

Content: _____

❑ **Naturalist/Environmental Product:** _____

Content: _____

❑ **Interpersonal Product:** _____

Content: _____

❑ **Intrapersonal Product:** _____

Content: _____

Materials/Resources Needed: _____

_____

_____

Individual Project Planning Menu

Name: _____

Unit of Study: _____

Date: _____ **Goal Date for Completion:** _____

Standards/Content: _____

_____

❑ **#1 Product:** _____

    Content: _____

❑ **#2 Product:** _____

    Content: _____

❑ **#3 Product:** _____

    Content: _____

❑ **#4 Product:** _____

    Content: _____

❑ **#5 Product:** _____

    Content: _____

❑ **#6 Product:** _____

    Content: _____

Materials/Resources Needed: _____

_____

_____

Group Project Plan

Names: _____

Unit of Study: _____

Standards/Content: _____

_____

Date: _____ **Goal Date for Completion:** _____

	Review by group (Initial here)

❑ **#1 Product:**
   Content:
   Group Member Assigned:	

❑ **#2 Product:**
   Content:
   Group Member Assigned:	

❑ **#3 Product:**
   Content:
   Group Member Assigned:	

❑ **#4 Product:**
   Content:
   Group Member Assigned:	

Materials/Resources Needed: _____

_____

_____

Project Self-Evaluation 1

Self-Evaluation for: _____ **Date:** _____

Directions: Complete the chart by answering the questions.

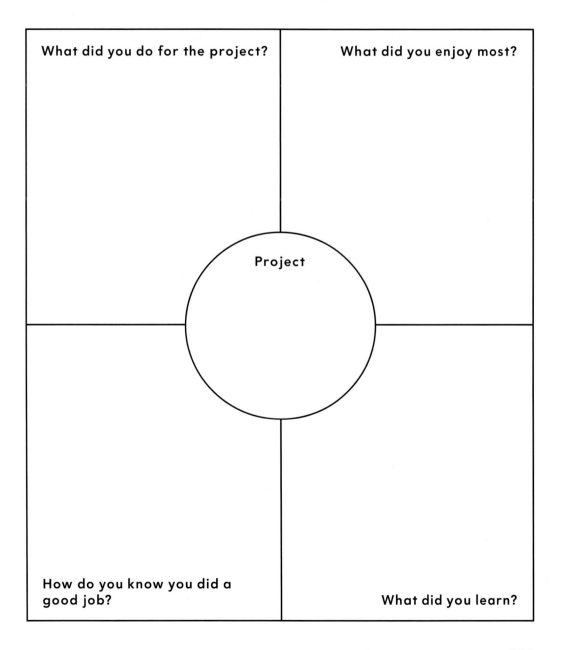

What did you do for the project?

What did you enjoy most?

Project

How do you know you did a good job?

What did you learn?

Project Self-Evaluation 2

Self-Evaluation for: _____ **Date:** _____

Directions: Complete the chart by answering the questions.

What steps did you take to complete the project?	What did you like about doing this project? What did you dislike about doing this project?
How do you know you did a good job?	**If you were to do this project again, what would you do the same? Differently?**

Project

Participation Evaluation 1

Name: _____ **Date:** _____

Activity: _____

Directions: Read the question. If the answer is yes, draw a smile on the *Yes* face. If the answer is no, draw a frown on the *No* face.

Did I share my ideas?

Did I help with the product?

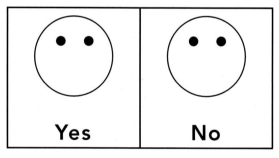

Did I finish on time?

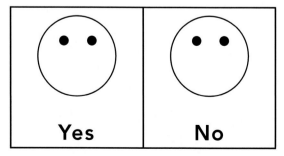

Participation Evaluation 2

Group Member Names: _____

Project: _____

My Name: _____

Directions: Place your initials on the line to show participation of yourself or the group member who is listed under "My Name."

Participated in discussion

Never   **Always**

Contributed original ideas

Never   **Always**

Helped create final project

Never   **Always**

Problem-Based Assessment Plan

Name: _____ **Date:** _____

Time Frame for Completing the Problem: _____

Directions: Complete the chart by answering the questions.

What is the problem?
What is your past experience with this problem?
What do you know about this problem?
How will you solve the problem?
What do you need to solve the problem?
How will you present your solution to the problem?

Daily Log

Content Area: _____

Name: _____ **Date:** _____

I will complete _____ **by** _____ .

Date	Concept/Activity	Score	Initials	Comments

Student signature: _____

Weekly Log

Name: _____   **Week:** _____

Monday = red
Tuesday = orange
Wednesday = yellow
Thursday = green
Friday = blue

Directions: Fill in the circles with the color that tells on what day you filled in the log. Then, write about what you worked on that day.

Formative/Summative Grade Book Using Mode Scores

Standard/Activity	M1.2 Prob & Stats	M1.2 Graphs Galore	M1.2 Chapter Test	M1.2 Problem Solver	M1.2 Data Project	MODE Score	M1.4 Angle Answers	M1.4 Ray Recollections	M1.4 Shapes Project	M1.4 3–D Replica	M1.4 Unit Test	MODE Score	Avg. Mode*
Students/Quality													

*Use only when one score can be added to a content-based report card

Assessment and Grading Self-Evaluation

Educator: _____ **School Year:** _____

A = Always   **S** = Sometimes   **N** = Never

In my classroom...

A   S   N

❑ ❑ ❑ the use of standards to understand key concepts is the focus of learning.

❑ ❑ ❑ multiple materials are provided for student research and creation of products.

❑ ❑ ❑ pre-assessments are administered at the beginning of the year as well as throughout the year.

❑ ❑ ❑ student differences are identified and studied as a basis for planning.

❑ ❑ ❑ assessment is diagnostic and ongoing in order to make instruction more responsive to students' needs.

❑ ❑ ❑ many learning-profile options are provided.

❑ ❑ ❑ students are assessed in multiple ways.

❑ ❑ ❑ many instructional groupings are used.

❑ ❑ ❑ students are often guided in making intelligence-based and interest-based learning choices.

❑ ❑ ❑ multi-option assignments are frequently used.

❑ ❑ ❑ assignments and activities are linked directly to standards.

❑ ❑ ❑ student readiness, interest, and learning profile shape instruction.

❑ ❑ ❑ criteria for quality work is considered when evaluating student products.

❑ ❑ ❑ formative assessments are evaluated but not included on the report card.

❑ ❑ ❑ summative assessment evaluations are the only scores that make it onto the report card.

❑ ❑ ❑ excellence is largely defined by individual growth from an identifiable starting point.

References Cited

Anderson, Lorin W., and David R. Krathwohl. 2000. *A Taxonomy for Learning, Teaching, and Assessing: A Revision of Bloom's Taxonomy of Educational Objectives*. Boston, MA: Allyn & Bacon.

Armstrong, Thomas. 1994. *Multiple Intelligences in the Classroom*. Alexandria, VA: ASCD.

Bandura, Albert. 1997. *Self-Efficacy: The Exercise of Control*. New York: W.H. Freeman.

Banta, Trudy W., Jon P. Lund, Karen E. Black, and Frances W. Oblander. 1996. *Assessment in Practice: Putting Principles to Work on College Campuses*. San Francisco, CA. Jossey-Bass Inc.

Benjamin, Amy. 2003. *Differentiated Instruction: A Guide for Elementary School Teachers*. Larchmont, NY: Eye on Education.

Bloom, Benjamin, and David R. Krathwohl. 1984. *Taxonomy of Educational Objectives*. Longman, NY: Longman Publishing Group.

Brooks, Ashley. 2004. "eHow | How to Videos, Articles & More—Discover the Expert in You." Accessed September 15, 2012. http://www.ehow.com/.

Bucher, Ingrid. 1987. "A Close Look at Vector Performance of Register-to-Register Vector Computers and a New Model." SIGMETRICS '87 Proceedings of the 1987 ACM SIGMETRICS Conference on Measurement and Modeling of Computer Systems.

Carter, Dave. 2001. "Assessment—Why We Do It How We Do It." Handout presented at a CEP Teaching Methodology Workshop. Accessed October 23, 2012. http://civiceducationproject.org/legacy /teachandlearn/doc/cartervarna.pdf.

Coffey, Heather. 2009. "Summative Assessment." Chapel Hill, NC: LEARN North Carolina. Accessed September 15, 2012. http://www.learnnc.org/lp/pages/5233.

Cuban, Larry. 2011. "Larry Cuban on School Reform and Classroom Practice: Data-Driven Instruction and the Practice of Teaching." Wordpress. Accessed September 15, 2012. http://larrycuban.wordpress.com/2011/05/12/data-driven-instruction-and-the-practice-of-teaching.

Culham, Ruth, and Amanda Wheeler. 2003. *Writing to Prompts in the Trait-Based Classroom Content Areas: Literature Response.* New York: Scholastic Inc.

DiPietro, Michele. 1995. "Using Cognitive Theories to Improve Teaching." *The Teaching Professor* (April): 3–4.

Education.com. 2012. "Glossary of Education: Weighted Scores." Accessed June 15. http://www.education.com/definition/weighted-scores.

FairTest: The National Center for Fair & Open Testing. 2008. "Transforming Student Assessment." Accessed June 16, 2012. http://www.fairtest.org/transforming-student-assessment.

Fisher, Doug, and Nancy Frey. 2007. *Checking for Understanding: Formative Assessment Techniques in Your Classroom.* Alexandria, VA: ASCD.

Fritz, Robert. 1989. *Path of Least Resistance: Learning to Become the Creative Force in Your Own Life.* New York: Random House.

Gallagher, Shelagh, Hillary Rosenthal, and William Stepien. 1993. "The Effects of Problem-Based Learning on Problem Solving." *Gifted Child Quarterly* 36 (4): 195–200.

Gardner, Howard. 1983. *Frames of Mind: The Theory of Multiple Intelligences.* New York: Basic Books.

———. 1999. *Intelligence Reframed: Multiple Intelligences for the 21st Century.* New York: Basic Books.

Glasser, William. 1969. *The Learning Pyramid.* Bethel, ME: National Training Laboratories.

Grassley, Chuck. 2005. "Grassley Continues Efforts to Help Gifted and Talented Students and Educators." http://www.grassley.senate.gov/news /Article.cfm?customel_dataPageID_1502=7036.

Hunter, Madeline. 1994. *Enhancing Teaching.* Upper Saddle River, NJ: Prentice Hall, Inc.

Lazear, David. 1999. *Multiple Intelligences Approaches to Assessment: Solving the Assessment Conundrum.* Tucson, AZ: Zephyr Press.

Marzano, Robert. 1994. "Lessons From the Field About Outcome-Based Performance Assessments." *Educational Leadership* 51 (6): 44–50.

———. 2000. *Transforming Classroom Grading.* Aurora, CO: McREL Institute.

O'Connor, Ken. 2002. *How to Grade for Learning: Linking Grades to Standards.* Second edition, Glenview, IL: LessonLab.

Pally, Regina. 1997. "How Brain Development Is Shaped by Genetic and Environmental Factors." *International Journal of Psycho-Analysis* (78): 587–593.

Pear, Joseph. 2001. *The Science of Learning.* Philadelphia, PA: Taylor & Francis.

Smutny, Joan Franklin. 1997. *Teaching Young Gifted Children in the Regular Classroom.* Minneapolis, MN: Free Spirit Publishing, Inc.

Soloman, Barbara, and Richard Felder. 1999. "Index of Learning Styles Questionnaire." Raleigh, NC: College of Engineering, North Carolina State University. Accessed September 15, 2012. http://www.engr.ncsu .edu/learningstyles/ilsweb.html.

Tomlinson, Carol Ann. 2007. "Learning to Love Assessment." *Educational Leadership* 65 (4): 8–13.

Tomlinson, Carol Ann, and M. Laybe Kalbfleish. 1998. "Teach Me, Teach My Brain: A Call for Differentiated Classrooms." *Educational Leadership* (November): 56 (3): 52–55.

Wormeli, Rick. 2007. *Differentiation: From Planning to Practice, Grades 6–12*. Portland, ME: Stenhouse Publishers.